BEST-LOVED BAKING COLLECTION™

Cake-Mix MAGIC

America's ★ Best
BRAND-NAME RECIPES®

Pictured on the front cover: Black Forest Cake *(page 48).*
Pictured on the back cover *(left to right):* Lemon Crumb Bars *(page 134)* and Cool and Minty Party Cake *(page 44).*

ISBN: 0-8487-2877-7

Library of Congress Control Number: 2004102740

Manufactured in China.

8 7 6 5 4 3 2 1

Microwave Cooking: Microwave ovens vary in wattage. Use the cooking times as guidelines and check for doneness before adding more time.

Preparation/Cooking Times: Preparation times are based on the approximate amount of time required to assemble the recipe before cooking, baking, chilling or serving. These times include preparation steps such as measuring, chopping and mixing. The fact that some preparations and cooking can be done simultaneously is taken into account. Preparation of optional ingredients and serving suggestions is not included.

Contents

enchanting
cakes

peach-pecan upside-down cake

1 can (8½ ounces) peach slices
⅓ cup packed brown sugar
2 tablespoons butter or margarine, melted
¼ cup chopped pecans
1 package (16 ounces) pound cake mix plus ingredients to prepare mix
½ teaspoon almond extract
Whipped cream (optional)

Slow Cooker Directions

1. Generously grease 7½-inch slow cooker bread-and-cake baking pan or casserole dish; set aside.

2. Drain peach slices, reserving 1 tablespoon juice. Combine reserved peach juice, brown sugar and butter in prepared baking pan. Arrange peach slices over brown sugar mixture. Sprinkle with pecans.

3. Prepare cake mix according to package directions; stir in almond extract. Spread over peaches. Cover pan. Make foil handles (see note) for easier removal of pan from slow cooker. Place pan in slow cooker. Cover; cook on HIGH 3 hours.

4. Use foil handles to remove pan from slow cooker. Cool, uncovered, on wire rack for 10 minutes. Run narrow spatula around side of pan; invert onto serving plate. Serve warm with whipped cream, if desired.

Makes 10 servings

note: To make foil handles, tear off three 18×2-inch strips heavy-duty aluminum foil or use regular foil folded to double thickness. Crisscross foil strips in spoke design and place pan on center of strips. Pull foil strips up and over pan.

Prep Time: 10 minutes
Cook Time: 3 hours

double chocolate snack cake →

    **1 package DUNCAN HINES® Moist Deluxe® Devil's Food
Cake Mix**
    1 cup white chocolate chips, divided
    ¹/₂ cup semisweet chocolate chips

1. Preheat oven to 350°F. Grease and flour 13×9-inch pan.

2. Prepare cake mix as directed on package. Stir in ¹/₂ cup white
chocolate chips and semisweet chocolate chips. Pour into prepared
pan. Bake at 350°F for 35 to 40 minutes or until toothpick inserted
in center comes out clean. Remove from oven; sprinkle top with
remaining ¹/₂ cup white chocolate chips. Serve warm or cool
completely in pan.   *Makes 12 to 16 servings*

serving suggestion: For a special dessert, serve cake warm with a
scoop of vanilla ice cream or whipped cream garnished with
additional chocolate chips.

fudgy peanut butter cake

    1 (18.25-ounce) box chocolate fudge cake mix
    2 eggs
  1¹/₂ cups plus ²/₃ cup water, divided
    1 (16-ounce) package chocolate fudge frosting mix
  **1¹/₄ cups SMUCKER'S® Chunky Natural Peanut Butter or JIF®
Chunky Peanut Butter**

Grease and flour 10-inch tube pan. In large bowl, blend cake mix, eggs
and 1¹/₂ cups water until moistened; mix as directed on cake mix
package. Pour batter into prepared pan.

In medium bowl, combine frosting mix, peanut butter and remaining
²/₃ cup water; blend until smooth. Spoon over batter in pan.

Bake in preheated 350°F oven 35 to 45 minutes or until top springs
back when touched lightly in center. Cool upright in pan 1 hour;
remove from pan. Cool completely.   *Makes 12 to 15 servings*

lemon crumb cake

**1 package DUNCAN HINES® Moist Deluxe® Lemon Supreme
Cake Mix**
3 eggs
1 1/3 cups water
1/3 cup vegetable oil
1 cup all-purpose flour
1/2 cup packed light brown sugar
1/2 teaspoon baking powder
1/2 cup butter or margarine

1. Preheat oven to 350°F. Grease and flour 13×9-inch pan.

2. Combine cake mix, eggs, water and oil in large mixing bowl. Beat at medium speed with electric mixer for 2 minutes. Pour into prepared pan. Combine flour, sugar and baking powder in small bowl. Cut in butter until crumbly. Sprinkle evenly over batter. Bake at 350°F for 35 to 40 minutes or until toothpick inserted in center comes out clean. Cool completely in pan.   *Makes 12 to 16 servings*

 Butter or margarine will cut more easily into the flour mixture if it is chilled. Use two knives or a pastry cutter to cut the mixture into the crumbs.

orange glow bundt cake

1 (18.25-ounce) package moist yellow cake mix
1 tablespoon grated orange peel
1 cup orange juice
$^1/_4$ cup granulated sugar
1 tablespoon TABASCO® brand Pepper Sauce
$1^3/_4$ cups confectioners' sugar

Preheat oven to 375°F. Grease 12-cup Bundt pan. Prepare cake mix according to package directions, adding orange peel to batter. Bake 35 to 40 minutes or until toothpick inserted in center of cake comes out clean.

Meanwhile, heat orange juice, granulated sugar and TABASCO® Sauce to boiling in 1-quart saucepan. Reduce heat to low; simmer, uncovered, 5 minutes. Remove from heat. Reserve $^1/_4$ cup orange juice mixture for glaze.

Remove cake from oven. With wooden skewer, poke holes in cake (in pan) in several places. Spoon remaining orange juice mixture over cake. Cool cake in pan 10 minutes. Carefully invert cake onto wire rack to cool completely.

Combine reserved $^1/_4$ cup orange juice mixture and confectioners' sugar in small bowl until smooth. Place cake on platter; spoon glaze over cake. Garnish with clusters of dried cranberries, mint leaves and grated orange peel, if desired. *Makes 12 servings*

fudge ribbon cake

1 (18.25-ounce) package chocolate cake mix
1 (8-ounce) package cream cheese, softened
2 tablespoons butter or margarine, softened
1 tablespoon cornstarch
1 (14-ounce) can EAGLE BRAND® Sweetened Condensed Milk
   (NOT evaporated milk)
1 egg
1 teaspoon vanilla extract
   Chocolate Glaze (recipe follows)

1. Preheat oven to 350°F. Grease and flour 13×9-inch baking pan. Prepare cake mix as package directs. Pour batter into prepared pan.

2. In small mixing bowl, beat cream cheese, butter and cornstarch until fluffy. Gradually beat in Eagle Brand. Add egg and vanilla; beat until smooth. Spoon evenly over cake batter.

3. Bake 40 minutes or until wooden pick inserted near center comes out clean. Cool. Prepare Chocolate Glaze and drizzle over cake. Store covered in refrigerator. *Makes 10 to 12 servings*

chocolate glaze: In small saucepan over low heat, melt 1 (1-ounce) square unsweetened or semi-sweet chocolate and 1 tablespoon butter or margarine with 2 tablespoons water. Remove from heat. Stir in ³/₄ cup powdered sugar and ¹/₂ teaspoon vanilla extract. Stir until smooth and well blended. Makes about ¹/₃ cup.

banana-coconut crunch cake

Cake

> 1 package DUNCAN HINES® Moist Deluxe® Banana Supreme Cake Mix
>
> 1 package (4-serving size) banana-flavor instant pudding and pie filling mix
>
> 1 can (16 ounces) fruit cocktail, in juices, undrained
>
> 4 eggs
>
> 1/4 cup vegetable oil
>
> 1 cup flaked coconut
>
> 1/2 cup chopped pecans
>
> 1/2 cup firmly packed brown sugar

Glaze

> 3/4 cup granulated sugar
>
> 1/2 cup butter or margarine
>
> 1/2 cup evaporated milk
>
> 1 1/3 cups flaked coconut

1. Preheat oven to 350°F. Grease and flour 13×9×2-inch pan.

2. For cake, combine cake mix, pudding mix, fruit cocktail with juice, eggs and oil in large bowl. Beat at medium speed with electric mixer for 4 minutes. Stir in 1 cup coconut. Pour into prepared pan. Combine pecans and brown sugar in small bowl. Stir until well mixed. Sprinkle over batter. Bake at 350°F for 45 to 50 minutes or until toothpick inserted in center comes out clean.

3. For glaze, combine granulated sugar, butter and evaporated milk in medium saucepan. Bring to a boil. Cook for 2 minutes, stirring occasionally. Remove from heat. Stir in 1 1/3 cups coconut. Pour over warm cake. Serve warm or at room temperature.

Makes 12 to 16 servings

hint: Assemble all ingredients and utensils together before beginning the recipe.

fantasy angel food cake

1 package DUNCAN HINES® Angel Food Cake Mix
Red and green food coloring
1 container DUNCAN HINES® Creamy Home-Style Cream
Cheese Frosting

1. Preheat oven to 350°F.

2. Prepare cake following package directions. Divide batter into thirds and place in 3 different bowls. Add a few drops red food coloring to one. Add a few drops green food coloring to another. Stir each until well blended. Leave the third one plain. Spoon pink batter into ungreased 10-inch tube pan. Cover with white batter and top with green batter. Bake and cool following package directions.

3. To make cream cheese glaze, heat frosting in microwave at HIGH (100% power) 20 to 30 seconds. Do not overheat. Stir until smooth. Set aside ¼ cup warm glaze. Spoon remaining glaze on top and sides of cake to completely cover. Divide remaining glaze in half and place in 2 different bowls. Add a few drops red food coloring to one. Add a few drops green food coloring to the other. Stir each until well blended. Using a teaspoon, drizzle green glaze around edge of cake so it will run down sides. Repeat with pink glaze. *Makes 16 servings*

hint: For marble cake, drop batter by spoonfuls, alternating colors frequently.

fudge cake with melba topping

Cake
>1 package DUNCAN HINES® Moist Deluxe® Dark Chocolate
>>Fudge Cake Mix
>
>Egg substitute product equal to 3 eggs
>
>$1\frac{1}{4}$ cups water
>
>$\frac{1}{2}$ cup vegetable oil

Raspberry Sauce
>1 package (12 ounces) frozen dry pack raspberries, thawed,
>>drained and juice reserved
>
>$\frac{1}{2}$ cup sugar
>
>2 teaspoons cornstarch
>
>$\frac{1}{2}$ teaspoon grated lemon peel
>
>1 can (29 ounces) sliced peaches in lite syrup, drained

1. Preheat oven to 350°F. Grease and flour 13×9×2-inch pan.

2. For cake, combine cake mix, egg substitute, water and oil in large bowl. Beat at medium speed with electric mixer for 2 minutes. Pour into prepared pan. Bake at 350°F for 35 to 40 minutes or until toothpick inserted in center comes out clean. Cool completely.

3. For raspberry sauce, combine reserved raspberry juice, sugar, cornstarch and lemon peel in medium saucepan. Bring to a boil. Reduce heat and cook until thickened, stirring constantly. Stir in reserved raspberries. Cool.

4. Cut cake into serving squares. Place several peach slices on top of cake square. Spoon raspberry sauce over peaches and cake. Serve immediately. *Makes 20 servings*

hint: To separate juice from raspberries in one step, allow berries to thaw at room temperature in a strainer placed over a bowl.

cappuccino cake

$^1/_2$ cup (3 ounces) semisweet chocolate chips
$^1/_2$ cup chopped hazelnuts, walnuts or pecans
1 (18.25-ounce) package yellow cake mix
$^1/_4$ cup instant espresso coffee powder
2 teaspoons ground cinnamon
1$^1/_4$ cups water
3 eggs
$^1/_3$ cup FILIPPO BERIO® Pure or Extra Light Tasting Olive Oil
Powdered sugar
1 (15-ounce) container ricotta cheese
2 teaspoons granulated sugar
Additional ground cinnamon

Preheat oven to 325°F. Grease 10-inch (12-cup) Bundt pan or 10-inch tube pan with olive oil. Sprinkle lightly with flour.

In small bowl, combine chocolate chips and hazelnuts. Spoon evenly into bottom of prepared pan.

In large bowl, combine cake mix, coffee powder and 2 teaspoons cinnamon. Add water, eggs and olive oil. Beat with electric mixer at low speed until dry ingredients are moistened. Beat at medium speed 2 minutes. Pour batter over topping in pan.

Bake 60 minutes or until toothpick inserted in center comes out clean. Cool on wire rack 15 minutes. Remove from pan. Place cake, fluted side up, on serving plate. Cool completely. Sprinkle with powdered sugar.

In medium bowl, combine ricotta cheese and granulated sugar. Sprinkle with cinnamon. Serve cheese mixture alongside slices of cake. Serve cake with cappuccino, espresso or your favorite coffee, if desired.

Makes 12 to 16 servings

strawberry stripe refrigerator cake

Cake

> 1 package DUNCAN HINES® Moist Deluxe® Classic White
>   Cake Mix
> 2 packages (10 ounces) frozen sweetened strawberry slices,
>   thawed

Topping

> 1 package (4-serving size) vanilla-flavor instant pudding and pie
>   filling mix
> 1 cup milk
> 1 cup whipping cream, whipped
>   Fresh strawberries for garnish (optional)

1. Preheat oven to 350°F. Grease and flour 13×9×2-inch pan.

2. For cake, prepare, bake and cool following package directions. Poke holes 1 inch apart in top of cake using handle of wooden spoon. Purée thawed strawberries with juice in blender or food processor. Spoon evenly over top of cake, allowing mixture to soak into holes.

3. For topping, combine pudding mix and milk in large bowl. Stir until smooth. Fold in whipped cream. Spread over cake. Decorate with fresh strawberries, if desired. Refrigerate at least 4 hours.

Makes 12 to 16 servings

variation: For a Neapolitan Refrigerator Cake, substitute Duncan Hines® Moist Deluxe® Devil's Food Cake Mix for the White Cake Mix and follow directions listed above.

fudgy banana oat cake

Topping
- 1 cup QUAKER® Oats (quick or old fashioned, uncooked)
- ½ cup firmly packed brown sugar
- ¼ cup (½ stick) margarine or butter, chilled

Filling
- 1 cup (6 ounces) semisweet chocolate pieces
- ⅔ cup sweetened condensed milk (not evaporated milk)
- 1 tablespoon margarine or butter

Cake
- 1 package (18.25 ounces) devil's food cake mix
- 1¼ cups mashed ripe bananas (about 3 large)
- ⅓ cup vegetable oil
- 3 eggs
- Banana slices (optional)
- Sweetened whipped cream (optional)

Heat oven to 350°F. Lightly grease bottom only of 13×9-inch baking pan. For topping, combine oats and brown sugar. Cut in margarine until mixture is crumbly; set aside.

For filling, in small saucepan, heat chocolate pieces, sweetened condensed milk and margarine over low heat until chocolate is melted, stirring occasionally. Remove from heat; set aside.

For cake, in large mixing bowl, combine cake mix, bananas, oil and eggs. Blend at low speed of electric mixer until dry ingredients are moistened. Beat at medium speed 2 minutes. Spread batter evenly into prepared pan. Drop filling mixture by teaspoonfuls evenly over batter. Sprinkle with reserved topping mixture. Bake 40 to 45 minutes or until cake pulls away from sides of pan and topping is golden brown. Cool cake in pan on wire rack. Cut into squares. Garnish with banana slices and sweetened whipped cream, if desired. *Makes 15 servings*

spice cake with fresh peach sauce

Cake

> 1 package DUNCAN HINES® Moist Deluxe® Spice Cake Mix
> 3 egg whites*
> 1¼ cups water
> ⅓ cup vegetable oil

Sauce

> 6 cups sliced fresh peaches
> 1 cup water
> ⅓ cup sugar
> ⅛ teaspoon ground cinnamon

Use ¾ cup egg substitute in place of egg whites, if desired.

1. Preheat oven to 350°F. Grease and flour 10-inch Bundt or tube pan.

2. For cake, place cake mix, egg whites, water and oil in large bowl. Beat at low speed with electric mixer until blended. Beat at medium speed 2 minutes. Pour into pan. Bake at 350°F for 42 to 47 minutes or until toothpick inserted in center comes out clean. Cool in pan 25 minutes. Invert onto serving plate. Cool completely. Dust with confectioners' sugar, if desired.

3. For sauce, combine peaches and water in large saucepan. Cook over medium heat 5 minutes. Reduce heat to low. Cover and simmer 10 minutes. Cool. Reserve ½ cup peach slices. Combine remaining peaches with any cooking liquid, sugar and cinnamon in blender or food processor. Process until smooth. Stir in reserved peach slices. To serve, spoon peach sauce over cake slices.   *Makes 12 to 16 servings*

note: The fresh peach sauce can be served either warm or chilled.

chocolate confection cake

1 package DUNCAN HINES® Moist Deluxe® Devil's Food
  Cake Mix

Filling

1 cup evaporated milk
1 cup granulated sugar
24 large marshmallows
1 package (14 ounces) flaked coconut

Topping

$1/2$ cup butter or margarine
$1/4$ cup plus 2 tablespoons milk
$1/3$ cup unsweetened cocoa powder
1 pound confectioners' sugar ($3^1/2$ to 4 cups)
1 teaspoon vanilla extract
$3/4$ cup sliced almonds

1. Preheat oven to 350°F. Grease and flour $15^1/2 \times 10^1/2 \times 1$-inch jelly-roll pan.

2. Prepare cake following package directions for original recipe. Pour into prepared pan. Bake at 350°F for 20 to 25 minutes or until toothpick inserted in center comes out clean.

3. For filling, combine evaporated milk and granulated sugar in large saucepan. Bring mixture to a boil. Add marshmallows and stir until melted. Stir in coconut. Spread on warm cake.

4. For topping, combine butter, milk and cocoa in medium saucepan. Stir on low heat until butter is melted. Add confectioners' sugar and vanilla extract, stirring until smooth. Pour over filling. Spread evenly to edges. Sprinkle with almonds. Cool completely.

Makes 20 to 24 servings

marbled chocolate sour cream cake

1 cup (6 ounces) NESTLÉ® TOLL HOUSE® Semi-Sweet Chocolate
    Morsels
1 package (18.5 ounces) yellow cake mix
4 eggs
³/₄ cup sour cream
¹/₂ cup vegetable oil
¹/₄ cup water
¹/₄ cup granulated sugar
    Powdered sugar (optional)

PREHEAT oven to 375°F. Grease 10-cup bundt or round tube pan.

MICROWAVE morsels in medium, uncovered, microwave-safe bowl on HIGH (100%) power for 1 minute. STIR. Morsels may retain some of their original shape. If necessary, microwave at additional 10- to 15-second intervals, stirring just until morsels are melted.

COMBINE cake mix, eggs, sour cream, vegetable oil, water and granulated sugar in large mixer bowl. Beat on low speed until moistened. Beat on high speed for 2 minutes.

STIR *2 cups* batter into melted chocolate. Alternately spoon batters into prepared pan, beginning and ending with yellow batter.

BAKE for 35 to 40 minutes or until wooden pick inserted in cake comes out clean. Cool in pan for 20 minutes; invert onto wire rack to cool completely. Dust with powdered sugar before serving.

Makes 20 servings

everyone's favorite e-z lemon cake

1 package (18¼ ounces) two-layer yellow or lemon cake mix
(without pudding mix preferred)
1 package (3.4 ounces) *instant* lemon pudding and pie
filling mix
4 eggs
1 cup water
⅓ cup vegetable oil
Grated peel and juice of 1 SUNKIST® lemon (3 tablespoons
juice)
E-Z Lemon Glaze (recipe follows)

In large bowl, combine cake mix, pudding mix, eggs, water, oil and
lemon juice with electric mixer at low speed 30 seconds. Beat at
medium speed 2 minutes longer. Stir in lemon peel. Pour batter into
well-greased and lightly floured Bundt pan or 10-inch tube pan.

Bake at 350°F for 50 to 60 minutes or until toothpick inserted in
center comes out clean. Cool on wire rack 15 minutes. With narrow
spatula or knife, loosen cake from tube and side; invert onto cake
plate. While still warm, pierce top all over with long two-prong fork or
wooden skewer. Spread top with half of E-Z Lemon Glaze. Cool
completely. Spoon remaining glaze over cake, allowing some to drizzle
over sides.   *Makes 16 servings*

e-z lemon glaze: In small bowl, combine 1 cup confectioners' sugar,
juice of ½ SUNKIST® lemon (1½ tablespoons) and ½ tablespoon
water.

*To get the most juice from a lemon, let it warm to room
temperature first. Then, just before squeezing, roll it on the
countertop with the palm of your hand, pressing down on
it as you roll.*

light-as-air
layer cakes

delicate white chocolate cake

1 package DUNCAN HINES® Moist Deluxe® White Cake Mix
1 package (4-serving size) vanilla-flavor instant pudding and pie
    filling mix
4 egg whites
1 cup water
$^1/_2$ cup vegetable oil
5 ounces finely chopped white chocolate
1 cup cherry preserves
8 drops red food coloring (optional)
2 cups whipping cream, chilled
2 tablespoons confectioners' sugar
    Maraschino cherries for garnish
1 ounce white chocolate shavings for garnish

1. Preheat oven to 350°F. Cut waxed paper circles to fit bottoms of three 9-inch round cake pans. Grease bottoms and sides of pans. Line with waxed paper circles.

2. Combine cake mix, pudding mix, egg whites, water and oil in large mixing bowl. Beat at medium speed with electric mixer for 2 minutes. Fold in chopped white chocolate. Pour into prepared pans. Bake at 350°F for 18 to 22 minutes or until toothpick inserted in center comes out clean. Cool in pans 15 minutes. Invert onto cooling racks. Peel off waxed paper. Cool completely.

3. Combine cherry preserves and food coloring, if desired. Stir to blend color.

4. Beat whipping cream in large bowl until soft peaks form. Add sugar gradually. Beat until stiff peaks form.

5. To assemble, place one cake layer on serving plate. Spread $^1/_2$ cup cherry preserves over cake. Place second cake layer on top. Spread with remaining preserves. Place third cake layer on top. Frost sides and top of cake with whipped cream. Decorate with maraschino cherries and white chocolate shavings. Refrigerate until ready to serve.

Makes 12 to 16 servings

chocolate toffee cream cake

> 1 package DUNCAN HINES® Moist Deluxe® Dark Chocolate
>   Fudge Cake Mix
> 3 eggs
> 1$^1/_3$ cups water
> $^1/_2$ cup vegetable oil
> 1 package (6 ounces) milk chocolate English toffee bits, divided
> 1 container (12 ounces) extra creamy non-dairy whipped
>   topping, thawed

1. Preheat oven to 350°F. Grease and flour two 9-inch round cake pans.

2. Blend cake mix, eggs, water and oil in large mixing bowl until moistened. Beat at medium speed with electric mixer for 4 minutes. Pour into prepared pans. Bake at 350°F for 30 to 33 minutes or until toothpick inserted in center comes out clean. Cool in pans 15 minutes.

3. Remove cakes from pans. Cool completely. Reserve $^1/_4$ cup toffee bits; fold remaining bits into whipped topping. Place one cake layer on serving plate; spread with $^3/_4$ cup topping mixture. Top with remaining layer. Frost sides and top with remaining topping mixture; garnish with reserved toffee bits. Refrigerate until ready to serve.

Makes 12 to 16 servings

hint: If chocolate toffee bits are not available, 4 chocolate covered toffee candy bars can be substituted. Process bars in a food processor until chopped.

carrot layer cake

Cake

    1 package **DUNCAN HINES®** Moist Deluxe® Classic Yellow
        Cake Mix
    4 eggs
    $\frac{1}{2}$ cup vegetable oil
    3 cups grated carrots
    1 cup finely chopped nuts
    2 teaspoons ground cinnamon

Cream Cheese Frosting

    1 package (8 ounces) cream cheese, softened
    $\frac{1}{4}$ cup butter or margarine, softened
    2 teaspoons vanilla extract
    4 cups confectioners' sugar

1. Preheat oven to 350°F. Grease and flour two 8- or 9-inch round baking pans.

2. For cake, combine cake mix, eggs, oil, carrots, nuts and cinnamon in large bowl. Beat at low speed with electric mixer until moistened. Beat at medium speed for 2 minutes. Pour into prepared pans. Bake at 350°F for 35 to 40 minutes or until toothpick inserted in centers comes out clean. Cool.

3. For cream cheese frosting, place cream cheese, butter and vanilla extract in large bowl. Beat at low speed until smooth and creamy. Add confectioners' sugar gradually, beating until smooth. Add more sugar to thicken, or milk or water to thin frosting, as needed. Fill and frost cooled cake. Garnish with whole pecans, if desired.

Makes 12 to 16 servings

refreshing lemon cake

1 package DUNCAN HINES® Moist Deluxe® Butter Recipe
  Golden Cake Mix
1 container DUNCAN HINES® Creamy Home-Style Cream
  Cheese Frosting
³/₄ cup purchased lemon curd
  Lemon drop candies, crushed for garnish (optional)

1. Preheat oven to 375°F. Grease and flour two 8- or 9-inch round cake pans.

2. Prepare, bake and cool cake following package directions for basic recipe.

3. To assemble, place one cake layer on serving plate. Place ¹/₄ cup Cream Cheese frosting in small resealable plastic bag. Snip off one corner. Pipe bead of frosting on top of layer around outer edge. Fill remaining area with lemon curd. Top with second cake layer. Spread remaining frosting on sides and top of cake. Garnish top of cake with crushed lemon candies, if desired.   *Makes 12 to 16 servings*

note: You can substitute Duncan Hines® Vanilla or Vanilla Buttercream frosting for the Cream Cheese frosting, if desired.

To crush the lemon drop candies, place them in a heavy resealable plastic food storage bag and seal. Then roll a rolling pin over the bag several times to crush them.

toasted almond supreme

1 package (about 18 ounces) devil's food cake mix, plus
    ingredients to prepare mix
1¼ cups strong coffee
2 cups cold whipping cream
¾ cup powdered sugar
2 tablespoons unsweetened cocoa powder
1½ teaspoons vanilla
½ cup seedless raspberry jam
1 cup sliced almonds, toasted*
Fresh raspberries for garnish (optional)

To toast almonds, spread in single layer on baking sheet. Bake in preheated 350°F oven 7 minutes or until golden brown, stirring frequently.

1. Lightly grease 2 (9-inch) round cake pans. Line bottoms with waxed paper. Prepare cake mix according to package directions, substituting coffee for 1¼ cups of liquid called for in directions. Divide batter evenly between prepared pans. Bake as directed. Cool in pans 15 minutes. Remove from pans; cool completely on wire racks.

2. For chocolate whipped cream, place whipping cream in medium bowl; beat at high speed of electric mixer 1½ to 2 minutes or until soft peaks form. Add powdered sugar, cocoa and vanilla; beat 15 to 20 seconds or until stiff peaks form. Cover with plastic wrap; refrigerate until ready to use.

3. Place one cake layer on serving plate. Stir raspberry jam until smooth. Spread ¼ cup jam over cake layer. Place remaining cake layer on top; spread remaining jam over cake layer. Frost cake with chocolate whipped cream.

4. Sprinkle some toasted almonds evenly over top of cake; press remaining almonds onto side of cake. Wrap loosely with plastic wrap; refrigerate until ready to serve. Just before serving, garnish with fresh raspberries, if desired. *Makes 12 servings*

ribbon cake

Cake

    1 **package DUNCAN HINES® Moist Deluxe® Classic White
Cake Mix**
    $1/4$ **cup flaked coconut, chopped**
    $1/4$ **cup natural pistachio nuts, finely chopped**
    Green food coloring
    $1/4$ **cup maraschino cherries, drained, finely chopped**
    Red food coloring

Frosting and Filling

    $3^1/4$ **cups confectioners' sugar**
    $1/2$ **cup shortening**
    $1/3$ **cup water**
    $1/4$ **cup powdered non-dairy creamer**
    $1^1/2$ **teaspoons vanilla extract**
    $1/4$ **teaspoon salt**
    Green food coloring
    $1/2$ **cup natural pistachio nuts, finely chopped**
    $3/4$ **cup cherry jam**
    **Whole maraschino cherries with stems and mint leaves, for
garnish**

1. Preheat oven to 350°F. Grease and flour three 8-inch square baking
pans.

2. For cake, prepare cake mix following package directions for basic
recipe. Mix $1^3/4$ cups batter and coconut in small bowl; set aside. Mix
$1^3/4$ cups batter, pistachio nuts and 5 drops green food coloring in small
bowl; set aside. Mix remaining batter, $1/4$ cup chopped maraschino
cherries and 2 drops red food coloring. Pour batters into separate pans.
Bake at 350°F for 18 minutes or until toothpick inserted in center
comes out clean. Cool following package directions. Trim cake edges.

3. For frosting, mix confectioners' sugar, shortening, water, creamer,
vanilla, salt and 5 drops green food coloring in bowl. Beat for
3 minutes at medium speed with electric mixer. Beat for 5 minutes at
high speed. Add more confectioners' sugar to thicken or water to thin
as needed. Add remaining $1/2$ cup pistachio nuts. Stir until blended.

4. To assemble, spread green and white cake layers with cherry jam.
Stack layers. Top with pink layer. Frost sides and top of cake. Garnish
with whole cherries and mint leaves. *Makes 12 to 16 servings*

cool and minty party cake

1 (14-ounce) can EAGLE BRAND® Sweetened Condensed Milk
  (NOT evaporated milk)
2 teaspoons peppermint extract
8 drops green food coloring, if desired
2 cups (1 pint) whipping cream, whipped (do not use non-dairy
  topping)
1 (18.25- or 18.5-ounce) package white cake mix
  Green crème de menthe liqueur
1 (8-ounce) container frozen non-dairy whipped topping,
  thawed

1. Line 9-inch round layer cake pan with aluminum foil. In large mixing bowl, combine Eagle Brand, peppermint extract and food coloring, if desired. Fold in whipped cream. Pour into prepared pan; cover. Freeze at least 6 hours or until firm.

2. Meanwhile, prepare and bake cake mix as package directs for two 9-inch round layers. Remove from pans; cool completely.

3. With fork, poke holes in cake layers, 1 inch apart, halfway through each layer. Spoon small amounts of liqueur into holes. Place one cake layer on serving plate; top with frozen Eagle Brand mixture, then second cake layer. Trim frozen layer even with edge of cake layers.

4. Frost quickly with whipped topping. Return to freezer at least 6 hours before serving. Garnish as desired. Freeze leftovers.

Makes one 9-inch cake

strawberry vanilla cake

1 package DUNCAN HINES® Moist Deluxe® French Vanilla
　 Cake Mix
1 container DUNCAN HINES® Creamy Home-Style Classic
　 Vanilla Frosting, divided
⅓ cup seedless strawberry jam
　 Fresh strawberries for garnish (optional)

1. Preheat oven to 350°F. Grease and flour two 8- or 9-inch round
cake pans.

2. Prepare, bake and cool cake following package directions for basic
recipe.

3. To assemble, place one cake layer on serving plate. Place ¼ cup
Vanilla frosting in small resealable plastic bag. Snip off one corner.
Pipe bead of frosting on top of layer around outer edge. Fill remaining
area with strawberry jam. Top with second cake layer. Spread
remaining frosting on side and top of cake. Decorate with fresh
strawberries, if desired.　　　　　　　　 *Makes 12 to 16 servings*

note: You can substitute Duncan Hines® Vanilla or Cream Cheese
frosting for the Vanilla Buttercream frosting, if desired.

*To make the strawberry jam easier to spread, place it
in a small bowl and stir vigorously with a spoon or small
wire whisk.*

black forest cake

1 package (about 18 ounces) chocolate cake mix plus
    ingredients to prepare mix
2 cans (20 ounces each) tart pitted cherries, undrained
1 cup granulated sugar
1/4 cup cornstarch
1 1/2 teaspoons vanilla
    Whipped Cream Frosting (recipe follows)

1. Preheat oven to 350°F. Grease and flour 2 (9-inch) round cake pans; set aside.

2. Prepare cake mix according to package directions. Divide batter between prepared pans.

3. Bake 30 to 35 minutes or until toothpicks inserted into centers come out clean. Cool in pans on wire racks 10 minutes. Remove from pans; cool completely on racks.

4. Meanwhile, drain cherries, reserving 1/2 cup juice. Combine reserved juice, cherries, sugar and cornstarch in 2-quart saucepan. Cook over low heat until thickened, stirring constantly. Remove from heat; stir in vanilla. Prepare Whipped Cream Frosting.

5. With long serrated knife, split each cooled cake layer horizontally in half. Crumble one split layer; set aside.

6. Reserve 1 1/2 cups frosting for decorating cake. Place one cake layer on serving plate. Spread with 1 cup frosting; top with 3/4 cup cherry topping. Top with second cake layer; repeat layers of frosting and cherry topping. Top with third cake layer.

7. Frost side of cake with remaining frosting. Pat reserved crumbs onto frosting on side of cake. Spoon reserved frosting into pastry bag fitted with star decorator tip. Pipe around top and bottom edges of cake. Spoon remaining cherry topping onto top of cake.

Makes one 3-layer cake

whipped cream frosting: Combine 3 cups cold whipping cream and 1/3 cup powdered sugar in chilled deep medium bowl. Beat at high speed of electric mixer until stiff peaks form.

banana fudge layer cake →

  1 package DUNCAN HINES® Moist Deluxe® Yellow Cake Mix
1¹/₃ cups water
  3 eggs
  ¹/₃ cup vegetable oil
  1 cup mashed ripe bananas (about 3 medium)
  1 container DUNCAN HINES® Chocolate Frosting

1. Preheat oven to 350°F. Grease and flour two 9-inch round cake pans.

2. Combine cake mix, water, eggs and oil in large bowl. Beat at low speed with electric mixer until moistened. Beat at medium speed 2 minutes. Stir in bananas.

3. Pour into prepared pans. Bake at 350°F for 28 to 31 minutes or until toothpick inserted in center comes out clean. Cool in pans 15 minutes. Remove from pans; cool completely.

4. Fill and frost cake with frosting. Garnish as desired.

Makes 12 to 16 servings

chocolate mayonnaise cake

1 box (18 ounces) chocolate cake mix
1 cup HELLMANN'S® or BEST FOODS® Mayonnaise
1 cup water
3 eggs
1 teaspoon ground cinnamon (optional)

1. Preheat oven to 350°F. Grease and lightly flour two 9-inch round cake pans; set aside.

2. In large bowl, with electric mixer at low speed, beat cake mix, mayonnaise, water, eggs and cinnamon 30 seconds. Beat at medium speed, scraping sides occasionally, 2 minutes. Pour into prepared pans.

3. Bake 30 minutes or until toothpick inserted in center comes out clean. On wire rack, cool 10 minutes; remove from pans and cool completely. Sprinkle, if desired, with confectioners' sugar or fill and frost.

Makes 12 servings

Prep Time: 5 minutes
Cook Time: 30 minutes

piña colada cake

Cake

1 package (about 18 ounces) white cake mix, plus ingredients to prepare mix

Rum Filling

$^1/_2$ cup cold whipping cream

$^1/_4$ cup dark rum

2 tablespoons powdered sugar

$^3/_4$ teaspoon vanilla

Whipped Topping

2 cups cold whipping cream

$^3/_4$ cup powdered sugar

2 teaspoons vanilla

Garnishes

1 fresh pineapple, peeled, cut in half lengthwise and cored

2 cups sweetened shredded coconut, toasted

1. Prepare and bake cake mix according to package directions using 2 (9-inch) round cake pans. Cool in pans on wire racks 15 minutes. Remove cakes from pans; cool completely.

2. For rum filling, combine all ingredients in small bowl until well blended. Cover with plastic wrap; refrigerate until needed.

3. For whipped topping, place 2 cups whipping cream in medium bowl; beat 1$^1/_2$ to 2 minutes or until soft peaks form. Add powdered sugar and vanilla; beat 15 seconds or until stiff peaks form. Cover with plastic wrap; refrigerate until needed.

4. Place pineapple cut side down on cutting board; slice very thinly. Place slices on paper towels; pat dry.

5. Place 1 cake layer on serving plate. Spread half of rum filling evenly over cake. Spread 1 cup whipped topping evenly over cake. Sprinkle with 1 cup coconut; top with remaining cake layer. Spread remaining rum filling evenly over cake. Spread remaining whipped topping evenly over top and side of cake; sprinkle top with remaining coconut.

6. Press pineapple slices around sides of cake vertically, overlapping slightly. Reserve any remaining pineapple slices for another use. Refrigerate cake until ready to serve. *Makes 12 servings*

elegant chocolate angel torte

⅓ cup HERSHEY'S Cocoa
1 package (about 16 ounces) angel food cake mix
2 envelopes (1.3 ounces each) dry whipped topping mix
1 cup cold nonfat milk
1 teaspoon vanilla extract
1 cup strawberry purée*
Strawberries

*Mash 2 cups sliced fresh strawberries (or frozen berries, thawed) in blender or food processor. Cover; blend until smooth. Purée should measure 1 cup.

1. Move oven rack to lowest position.

2. Sift cocoa over dry cake mix in large bowl; stir to blend. Proceed with mixing cake as directed on package. Bake and cool as directed for 10-inch tube pan. Carefully run knife along side of pan to loosen cake; remove from pan. Using serrated knife, slice cake horizontally into four layers.

3. Prepare whipped topping mix as directed on package, using 1 cup nonfat milk and 1 teaspoon vanilla. Fold in strawberry purée.

4. Place bottom cake layer on serving plate; spread with ⅓ of strawberry topping. Set next cake layer on top; spread with ⅓ of topping. Continue layering cake and topping, ending with cake layer. Garnish with strawberries. Refrigerate until ready to serve. Slice cake with sharp serrated knife, cutting with gentle sawing motion. Cover; refrigerate leftover cake. *Makes about 16 servings*

Prep Time: 30 minutes
Bake Time: 45 minutes
Cool Time: 2 hours

chocolate dream torte

1 package DUNCAN HINES® Moist Deluxe® Dark Chocolate
    Fudge Cake Mix
1 (6-ounce) package semisweet chocolate chips, melted
1 (8-ounce) container frozen non-dairy whipped topping,
    thawed, divided
1 container DUNCAN HINES® Creamy Home-Style Milk
    Chocolate Frosting
3 tablespoons finely chopped dry roasted pistachios

1. Preheat oven to 350°F. Grease and flour two 9-inch round cake
pans.

2. Prepare, bake and cool cake as directed on package for basic recipe.

3. For chocolate hearts garnish, spread melted chocolate to ⅛-inch
thickness on waxed paper-lined baking sheet. Cut shapes with heart
cookie cutter when chocolate begins to set. Refrigerate until firm. Push
out heart shapes. Set aside.

4. To assemble, split each cake layer in half horizontally. Place one
split cake layer on serving plate. Spread one-third of whipped topping
on top. Repeat with remaining layers and whipped topping, leaving
top plain. Frost sides and top with frosting. Sprinkle pistachios on top.
Position chocolate hearts by pushing points down into cake.
Refrigerate until ready to serve.   *Makes 12 to 16 servings*

chocolate strawberry dream torte: Omit semisweet chocolate chips
and chopped pistachios. Proceed as directed through step 2. Fold
1½ cups chopped fresh strawberries into whipped topping in large
bowl. Assemble as directed, filling torte with strawberry mixture and
frosting with Milk Chocolate frosting. Garnish cake with strawberry
fans and mint leaves, if desired.

celebration pumpkin cake →

 1 package (about 18 ounces) spice cake mix
 1 can (16 ounces) pumpkin
 3 eggs
 ¼ cup butter, softened
 1½ containers (16 ounces each) cream cheese frosting
 ⅓ cup caramel topping
    Pecan halves for garnish

Preheat oven to 350°F. Grease and flour 3 (9-inch) round cake pans. Combine cake mix, pumpkin, eggs and butter in large bowl; beat with electric mixer at medium speed 2 minutes. Divide batter evenly among prepared pans. Bake 20 to 25 minutes or until toothpicks inserted in centers come out clean. Cool in pans on wire rack for 5 minutes. Remove from pans; cool completely.

Place one cake layer on serving plate; cover with frosting. Repeat layers, ending with frosting. Frost side of cake. Spread caramel topping over top of cake, letting some caramel drip down side. Garnish with pecan halves.

Makes 16 servings

mocha fudge cake

 1 package DUNCAN HINES® Moist Deluxe® Butter Recipe Fudge
    Cake Mix
 1 cup hot fudge ice cream topping
 1 tablespoon instant coffee granules
 4 cups frozen non-dairy whipped topping, thawed, divided

1. Preheat oven to 375°F. Grease and flour two 9-inch round cake pans.

2. Prepare, bake and cool cake as directed on package.

3. Combine hot fudge topping and coffee in medium saucepan. Heat until coffee crystals are dissolved. Cool. Fold 2 cups whipped topping into fudge topping mixture. Refrigerate 30 minutes.

4. Place one cake layer on serving plate. Spread with 1 cup filling. Top with second cake layer. Add remaining 2 cups whipped topping to remaining filling. Frost top and sides of cake with topping mixture.

Makes 12 to 16 servings

magical
desserts

hot fudge sundae cake

1 package DUNCAN HINES® Moist Deluxe® Dark Chocolate
    Fudge Cake Mix
$^1/_2$ gallon brick vanilla ice cream

Fudge Sauce
    1 can (12 ounces) evaporated milk
  1$^1/_4$ cups sugar
    4 squares (1 ounce each) unsweetened chocolate
  $^1/_4$ cup butter or margarine
  1$^1/_2$ teaspoons vanilla extract
  $^1/_4$ teaspoon salt
    Whipped cream and maraschino cherries for garnish

1. Preheat oven to 350°F. Grease and flour 13×9×2-inch pan. Prepare, bake and cool cake following package directions.

2. Remove cake from pan. Split cake in half horizontally. Place bottom layer back in pan. Cut ice cream into even slices and place evenly over bottom cake layer (use all the ice cream). Place remaining cake layer over ice cream. Cover and freeze.

3. For fudge sauce, combine evaporated milk and sugar in medium saucepan. Stir constantly on medium heat until mixture comes to a rolling boil. Boil and stir for 1 minute. Add unsweetened chocolate and stir until melted. Beat over medium heat until smooth. Remove from heat. Stir in butter, vanilla extract and salt.

4. Cut cake into serving squares. For each serving, place cake square on plate; spoon hot fudge sauce on top. Garnish with whipped cream and maraschino cherry. *Makes 12 to 16 servings*

note: Fudge sauce may be prepared ahead and refrigerated in tightly sealed jar. Reheat when ready to serve.

rich pumpkin cheesecake

Crust

    1 package DUNCAN HINES® Moist Deluxe® Spice Cake Mix
    $\frac{1}{2}$ cup butter or margarine, melted

Filling

    3 packages (8 ounces each) cream cheese, softened
    1 can (14 ounces) sweetened condensed milk
    1 can (16 ounces) solid pack pumpkin
    4 eggs
    1 tablespoon pumpkin pie spice

Topping

    1 package (2$\frac{1}{2}$ ounces) sliced almonds
    2 cups whipping cream, chilled
    $\frac{1}{4}$ cup sugar

1. Preheat oven to 375°F.

2. For crust, combine cake mix and melted butter in large bowl; press into bottom of *ungreased* 10-inch springform pan.

3. For filling, combine cream cheese and sweetened condensed milk in large bowl. Beat with electric mixer at high speed 2 minutes. Add pumpkin, eggs and pumpkin pie spice. Beat at high speed 1 minute. Pour over prepared crust in pan. Bake at 375°F for 65 to 70 minutes or until set. Cool completely on rack. Refrigerate 2 hours. Loosen cake from side of pan; remove side of pan.

4. For topping, preheat oven to 300°F. Toast almonds on baking sheet at 300°F for 4 to 5 minutes or until fragrant and light golden brown. Cool completely. Beat whipping cream in medium bowl with electric mixer on high speed until soft peaks form. Gradually add sugar; beat until stiff peaks form. Spread over top of chilled cake. Garnish with toasted almonds. Refrigerate until ready to serve.

Makes 8 to 12 servings

note: To prepare in 13×9×2-inch pan, bake at 350°F 35 minutes or until set.

blueberry angel food cake rolls

1 package DUNCAN HINES® Angel Food Cake Mix
¼ cup confectioners' sugar plus additional for dusting
1 can (21 ounces) blueberry pie filling
   Mint leaves for garnish (optional)

1. Preheat oven to 350°F. Line two 15½×10½×1-inch jelly-roll pans with aluminum foil.

2. Prepare cake mix as directed on package. Divide and spread evenly into prepared pans. Cut through batter with knife or spatula to remove large air bubbles. Bake at 350°F for 15 minutes or until set. Invert cakes at once onto clean, lint-free dish towels dusted with sugar. Remove foil carefully. Roll up each cake with towel jelly-roll fashion, starting at short end. Cool completely.

3. Unroll cakes. Spread about 1 cup blueberry pie filling to within 1 inch of edges on each cake. Reroll and place seam-side down on serving plate. Dust with ¼ cup sugar. Garnish with mint leaves, if desired.   *Makes 2 cakes (8 servings each)*

variation: For a change in flavor, substitute cherry pie filling for the blueberry pie filling.

 The best way to cut angel food cake is to use a long serrated knife and a gentle, back and forth sawing motion. This prevents the cake from getting crushed by the knife.

dump cake →

1 can (20 ounces) crushed pineapple with juice, undrained
1 can (21 ounces) cherry pie filling
1 package DUNCAN HINES® Moist Deluxe® Yellow Cake Mix
1 cup chopped pecans or walnuts
1/2 cup butter or margarine, cut into thin slices

1. Preheat oven to 350°F. Grease 13×9-inch pan.

2. Dump pineapple with juice into prepared pan. Spread evenly. Dump in pie filling. Spread evenly. Sprinkle cake mix evenly over cherry layer. Sprinkle pecans over cake mix. Dot with butter. Bake at 350°F for 50 minutes or until top is lightly browned. Serve warm or at room temperature.   *Makes 12 to 16 servings*

note: You can use Duncan Hines® Moist Deluxe® Pineapple Supreme Cake Mix in place of Moist Deluxe® Yellow Cake Mix.

hot fudge pudding cake

1 package DUNCAN HINES® Moist Deluxe® Devil's Food
    Cake Mix
2 eggs
1 cup water
1 cup chopped pecans
1/2 cup granulated sugar
1/2 cup packed brown sugar
2 tablespoons unsweetened cocoa powder
1 cup boiling water
    Whipped topping for garnish

1. Preheat oven to 350°F. Grease and flour 13×9-inch pan.

2. Combine cake mix, eggs and water in large mixing bowl. Beat at medium speed with electric mixer for 2 minutes. Stir in pecans. Pour into prepared pan.

3. Combine granulated sugar, brown sugar and cocoa in small bowl. Sprinkle over batter. Pour boiling water over all. *Do not stir.* Bake at 350°F for 45 minutes or until toothpick inserted in center halfway to bottom comes out clean. Serve warm with whipped topping.

Makes 12 to 16 servings

decadent chocolate delight →

1 package (about 18 ounces) chocolate cake mix
8 ounces sour cream
1 cup chocolate chips
1 cup water
4 eggs
¾ cup vegetable oil
1 package (4-serving size) instant chocolate pudding and pie filling mix

Slow Cooker Directions

1. Lightly grease inside of slow cooker.

2. Combine all ingredients in large bowl. Pour into slow cooker. Cover; cook on LOW 6 to 8 hours or on HIGH 3 to 4 hours. Serve hot or warm with ice cream. *Makes 12 servings*

creamy banana toffee dessert

1 package DUNCAN HINES® Moist Deluxe® Butter Recipe Golden Cake Mix
1 package (4-serving size) banana cream-flavor instant pudding and pie filling mix
1½ cups milk
1 container (8 ounces) frozen non-dairy whipped topping, thawed
3 medium bananas, sliced
¾ cup English toffee bits

1. Preheat oven to 375°F. Grease and flour 10-inch tube pan.

2. Prepare, bake and cool cake as directed on package. Meanwhile, combine pudding mix and milk in medium bowl. Chill 5 minutes. Fold in whipped topping. Chill while cake cools.

3. To assemble, cut cake into 12 slices. Place 6 cake slices in 3-quart clear glass bowl. Top with half of bananas, pudding and toffee bits. Repeat layering. Chill until ready to serve. *Makes 12 to 14 servings*

boston cream pie

**1 package DUNCAN HINES® Moist Deluxe® Classic Yellow
   Cake Mix**
4 containers (3¹/₂ ounces each) ready-to-eat vanilla pudding
1 container DUNCAN HINES® Chocolate Frosting

1. Preheat oven to 350°F. Grease and flour two 8- or 9-inch round pans.

2. Prepare, bake and cool cake following package directions for basic recipe.

3. To assemble, place each cake layer on serving plate. Split layers in half horizontally. Spread contents of 2 containers of vanilla pudding on bottom layer of one cake. Place top layer on filling. Repeat for second cake layer. Remove lid and foil top of Chocolate frosting container. Heat in microwave oven at HIGH (100% power) 25 to 30 seconds. Stir. (Mixture should be thin.) Spread half the chocolate glaze over top of each cake. Refrigerate until ready to serve.

Makes 12 to 16 servings

note: For a richer flavor, substitute Duncan Hines® Butter Recipe Golden cake mix in place of Yellow cake mix.

To cut a cake horizontally in half, remove it from the pan and place on a flat surface. Measure the cake with a ruler and mark a cutting line with toothpicks. Cut through the cake with a long serrated knife, just above the toothpicks.

punch bowl party cake →

1 package (about 18 ounces) yellow cake mix plus ingredients
    to prepare mix
1 package (4-serving size) instant vanilla pudding and pie
    filling mix plus ingredients to prepare mix
2 cans (21 ounces each) cherry pie filling
1 cup chopped pecans
1 container (12 ounces) frozen nondairy whipped topping,
    thawed

1. Prepare cake mix and bake according to package directions for
13×9-inch cake; cool completely.

2. Prepare pudding mix according to package directions.

3. Crumble ¹/₂ of cake into bottom of small punch bowl. Cover with
¹/₂ of pudding.

4. Reserve a few cherries from one can of cherry pie filling for garnish.
Top pudding with layers of cherry pie filling, pecans and whipped
topping.

5. Repeat layers, using remaining cake, pudding and cherry pie filling.
Top with remaining pecans and whipped topping. Garnish with
reserved cherries. *Makes 1 cake*

kahlúa® chocolate-mint trifle

1 chocolate cake mix (without pudding)
1 cup KAHLÚA® Liqueur
2 boxes (4-serving size) instant chocolate pudding
3¹/₂ cups milk
3 cups whipped topping
  Peppermint candy, crushed

Prepare, bake and cool cake in 13×9-inch baking pan according to
package directions. Poke holes in cake with fork; pour Kahlúa® over
top. Refrigerate overnight. Cut cake into cubes.

Prepare pudding mix with milk in large bowl according to package
directions. Layer in large clear glass trifle dish or glass bowl ¹/₃ each of
cake cubes, pudding, whipped topping and candy. Repeat layers two
more times. Refrigerate leftovers. *Makes about 18 servings*

chocolate chip cheesecake

1 package DUNCAN HINES® Moist Deluxe® Devil's Food
    Cake Mix
$1/2$ cup vegetable oil
3 packages (8 ounces each) cream cheese, softened
$1^1/2$ cups granulated sugar
1 cup sour cream
$1^1/2$ teaspoons vanilla extract
4 eggs, lightly beaten
$3/4$ cup mini semisweet chocolate chips, divided
1 teaspoon all-purpose flour

1. Preheat oven to 350°F. Grease 10-inch springform pan.

2. Combine cake mix and oil in large bowl. Mix well. Press onto bottom of prepared pan. Bake at 350°F for 22 to 25 minutes or until set. Remove from oven. *Increase oven temperature to 450°F.*

3. Place cream cheese in large mixing bowl. Beat at low speed with electric mixer, adding sugar gradually. Add sour cream and vanilla extract, mixing until blended. Add eggs, mixing only until incorporated. Toss $1/2$ cup chocolate chips with flour. Fold into cream cheese mixture. Pour filling onto crust. Sprinkle with remaining $1/4$ cup chocolate chips. Bake at 450°F for 5 to 7 minutes. *Reduce oven temperature to 250°F.* Bake at 250°F for 60 to 65 minutes or until set. Loosen cake from side of pan with knife or spatula. Cool completely in pan on cooling rack. Refrigerate until ready to serve. Remove side of pan.

Makes 12 to 16 servings

hint: Place pan of water on bottom shelf of oven during baking to prevent cheesecake from cracking.

berry cobbler cake

2 cups (1 pint) fresh or frozen berries (blueberries, blackberries, and/or raspberries)
1 package (1-layer size) yellow cake mix
1 teaspoon ground cinnamon
1 egg
1 cup water, divided
¼ cup sugar
1 tablespoon cornstarch
Ice cream (optional)

1. Preheat oven to 375°F.

2. Place berries in 9×9-inch baking pan; set aside.

3. Combine cake mix and cinnamon in large bowl. Add egg and ¼ cup water; stir to combine. Spoon over berries.

4. Combine sugar and cornstarch in small bowl. Stir in remaining ¾ cup water until sugar mixture dissolves; pour over cake batter and berry mixture.

5. Bake 40 to 45 minutes or until lightly browned. Serve at room temperature or warm with ice cream, if desired.   *Makes 6 servings*

Use frozen berries without thawing them first. Thawed berries do not hold their shape, so they are best used for cooking and puréeing.

deep dish mocha tiramisu

    1 (14-ounce) can EAGLE BRAND® Sweetened Condensed Milk
        (NOT evaporated milk), divided
    1 (18¼-ounce) package chocolate cake mix with pudding
    1 cup water
    2 eggs
    ½ cup vegetable oil
        Creamy Coffee Filling (recipe follows)
        Espresso Sauce (page 80)
    ½ cup coffee liqueur
        Chocolate-covered coffee beans

1. Preheat oven to 350°F. Grease 5 (8-inch) round cake pans. Reserve ¼ cup Eagle Brand for Creamy Coffee Filling.

2. In large mixing bowl, beat ¾ cup Eagle Brand, cake mix, water, eggs and oil until blended. Pour 1 cup batter into each prepared pan.

3. Bake 13 to 14 minutes. Cool in pans on wire racks 10 minutes. Remove from pans; cool completely on wire racks. Prepare Creamy Coffee Filling and Espresso Sauce.

4. Brush each cake layer evenly with liqueur. Place 1 cake layer in 4-quart trifle dish or bowl; top with 1½ cups Creamy Coffee Filling. Drizzle with ½ cup Espresso Sauce. Repeat procedure with remaining cake layers, 1 cup chocolate filling, and ¼ cup sauce, ending with cake layer. Garnish with chocolate-covered coffee beans. Chill. Store covered in refrigerator.
Makes 12 servings

creamy coffee filling

    ¼ cup reserved EAGLE BRAND® Sweetened Condensed Milk
        (NOT evaporated milk)
    1 (8-ounce) package cream cheese, softened
    2 tablespoons coffee liqueur
    1½ cups cold whipping cream

In large mixing bowl, beat first 3 ingredients until blended, about 4 minutes. Add whipping cream and beat until stiff peaks form. Chill, if desired.
Makes 4½ cups filling

continued on page 80

espresso sauce

    1 cup water
    ¹/₂ cup ground espresso
    1 (14-ounce) can EAGLE BRAND® Sweetened Condensed Milk
       (NOT evaporated milk)
    ¹/₄ cup (¹/₂ stick) butter or margarine

In small saucepan over medium heat, bring 1 cup water and ground espresso to a boil. Remove from heat and let stand 5 minutes. Pour mixture through fine wire-mesh strainer; discard grounds. In small saucepan over medium heat, combine espresso and Eagle Brand. Bring to a boil. Remove from heat, stir in butter. Cool.

Makes 1¹/₄ cups sauce

pumpkin cheesecake bars

    1 (16-ounce) package pound cake mix
    3 eggs, divided
    2 tablespoons butter or margarine, melted
    4 teaspoons pumpkin pie spice, divided
    1 (8-ounce) package cream cheese, softened
    1 (14-ounce) can EAGLE BRAND® Sweetened Condensed Milk
       (NOT evaporated milk)
    1 (15-ounce) can pumpkin
    ¹/₂ teaspoon salt
    1 cup chopped nuts

1. Preheat oven to 350°F. In large mixing bowl, beat cake mix, 1 egg, butter and 2 teaspoons pumpkin pie spice on low speed of electric mixer until crumbly. Press onto bottom of ungreased 15×10×1-inch jelly-roll pan.

2. In large mixing bowl, beat cream cheese until fluffy. Gradually beat in Eagle Brand until smooth. Beat in remaining 2 eggs, pumpkin, remaining 2 teaspoons pumpkin pie spice and salt; mix well. Pour over crust; sprinkle with nuts.

3. Bake 30 to 35 minutes or until set. Cool. Chill; cut into bars. Store covered in refrigerator.

Makes 4 dozen bars

creamy eggnog dessert

Crust

    1 package DUNCAN HINES® Moist Deluxe® Swiss Chocolate or
        German Chocolate Cake Mix
    1/2 cup (1 stick) butter or margarine, melted
    1/2 cup chopped pecans

Filling

    1 package (8 ounces) cream cheese, softened
    1 cup granulated sugar
    1 container (12 ounces) frozen whipped topping, thawed,
        divided

Topping

    2 packages (4-serving size each) French vanilla-flavor instant
        pudding and pie filling mix
    3 cups cold milk
    1/4 teaspoon rum extract
    1/4 teaspoon ground nutmeg

1. Preheat oven to 350°F.

2. For crust, combine cake mix, melted butter and pecans in large
bowl. Reserve 1/2 cup mixture. Press remaining mixture onto bottom
of *ungreased* 13×9-inch pan. Bake 15 to 20 minutes or until surface
is firm. Cool. Toast reserved 1/2 cup mixture on cookie sheet 3 to
4 minutes, stirring once. Cool completely. Break lumps with fork to
make small crumbs.

3. For filling, combine cream cheese and sugar in large bowl; beat
until smooth. Stir in 1 cup whipped topping. Spread over cooled crust.
Refrigerate.

4. For topping, combine pudding mix and milk; beat 1 minute. Add
rum extract and nutmeg. Spread over cheese layer. Spread remaining
whipped topping over pudding layer. Sprinkle with reserved crumbs.
Refrigerate at least 2 hours.   *Makes 12 to 16 servings*

pumpkin pie crunch

    1 can (16 ounces) solid pack pumpkin
    1 can (12 ounces) evaporated milk
    3 eggs
  1½ cups sugar
    4 teaspoons pumpkin pie spice
   ½ teaspoon salt
    1 package DUNCAN HINES® Moist Deluxe® Classic Yellow
       Cake Mix
    1 cup chopped pecans
    1 cup butter or margarine, melted
      Whipped topping

1. Preheat oven to 350°F. Grease bottom only of 13×9×2-inch pan.

2. Combine pumpkin, evaporated milk, eggs, sugar, pumpkin pie spice and salt in large bowl. Pour into prepared pan. Sprinkle dry cake mix evenly over pumpkin mixture. Top with pecans. Drizzle with melted butter. Bake at 350°F for 50 to 55 minutes or until golden. Cool completely. Serve with whipped topping. Refrigerate leftovers.

Makes 16 to 20 servings

note: For a richer flavor, try using Duncan Hines® Moist Deluxe® Butter Recipe Golden Cake Mix.

 If you do not have 4 teaspoons pumpkin pie spice, substitute 2 teaspoons ground cinnamon, 1 teaspoon ground ginger and ½ teaspoon each ground allspice and ground nutmeg.

rum and spumone layered torte

        1 package (about 18 ounces) moist butter recipe yellow
            cake mix
        3 eggs
        1/2 cup butter, softened
        1/3 cup plus 2 teaspoons rum, divided
        1/3 cup water
        1 quart spumone ice cream, softened
        1 cup cold whipping cream
        1 tablespoon powdered sugar
        Chopped mixed candied fruit
        Red and green sugars for decorating (optional)

Preheat oven to 375°F. Grease and flour 15½×10½×1-inch jelly-roll pan. Combine cake mix, eggs, butter, 1/3 cup rum and water in large bowl. Beat with electric mixer at low speed until moistened. Beat at high speed 4 minutes. Pour evenly into prepared pan.

Bake 20 to 25 minutes or until toothpick inserted in center comes out clean. Cool in pan 10 minutes. Turn out of pan onto wire rack; cool completely.

Cut cake into three 10×5-inch pieces. Place one cake layer on serving plate. Spread with half the softened ice cream. Cover with second cake layer. Spread with remaining ice cream. Place remaining cake layer on top. Gently push down. Wrap cake in plastic wrap and freeze at least 4 hours.

Just before serving, combine cream, powdered sugar and remaining 2 teaspoons rum in small chilled bowl. Beat at high speed with chilled beaters until stiff peaks form. Remove cake from freezer. Spread thin layer of whipped cream mixture over top of cake. Place star tip in pastry bag; fill with remaining whipped cream mixture. Pipe rosettes around outer top edges of cake. Place candied fruit in narrow strip down center of cake. Sprinkle colored sugars over rosettes, if desired. Serve immediately. *Makes 8 to 10 servings*

trifle spectacular

1 package DUNCAN HINES® Moist Deluxe® Devil's Food
    Cake Mix
1 can (14 ounces) sweetened condensed milk
1 cup cold water
1 package (4-serving size) vanilla-flavor instant pudding and
    pie filling mix
2 cups whipping cream, whipped
2 tablespoons orange juice, divided
2½ cups sliced fresh strawberries, divided
1 pint fresh raspberries, divided
2 kiwifruit, peeled and sliced, divided
1½ cups frozen whipped topping, thawed for garnish
    Mint leaves for garnish (optional)

1. Preheat oven to 350°F. Grease and flour two 9-inch round cake pans.

2. Prepare, bake and cool cake following package directions for original recipe. Cut one cake layer into 1-inch cubes. Freeze other cake layer for later use.

3. Combine sweetened condensed milk and water in large bowl. Stir until blended. Add pudding mix. Beat until thoroughly blended. Chill 5 minutes. Fold whipped cream into pudding mixture.

4. To assemble, spread 2 cups pudding mixture into 3-quart trifle dish (or 3-quart clear glass bowl with straight sides). Arrange half the cake cubes over pudding mixture. Sprinkle with 1 tablespoon orange juice. Layer with 1 cup strawberry slices, half the raspberries and one-third of kiwifruit slices. Repeat layers. Top with remaining pudding mixture. Garnish with whipped topping, remaining ½ cup strawberry slices, kiwifruit slices and mint leaves, if desired.   *Makes 10 to 12 servings*

hint: Since the different layers contribute to the beauty of this recipe, arrange the fruit pieces to show attractively along the sides of the trifle dish.

mystifying miniatures

caramel apple cupcakes

1 package (about 18 ounces) butter recipe yellow cake mix plus
    ingredients to prepare mix
1 cup chopped dried apples
    Caramel Frosting (recipe follows)
    Chopped nuts (optional)

1. Preheat oven to 375°F. Line 24 regular-size (2½-inch) muffin pan cups with paper liners; set aside.

2. Prepare cake mix according to package directions. Stir in apples. Spoon batter into prepared muffin cups.

3. Bake 15 to 20 minutes or until toothpicks inserted into centers come out clean. Cool in pan on wire racks 10 minutes. Remove cupcakes to racks; cool completely.

4. Prepare Caramel Frosting. Frost cupcakes; sprinkle cupcakes with nuts, if desired. *Makes 24 cupcakes*

caramel frosting

3 tablespoons butter
1 cup packed brown sugar
½ cup evaporated milk
⅛ teaspoon salt
3¾ cups powdered sugar
¾ teaspoon vanilla

1. Melt butter in 2-quart saucepan. Stir in brown sugar, evaporated milk and salt. Bring to a boil, stirring constantly. Remove from heat; cool to lukewarm.

2. Beat in powdered sugar until frosting is of spreading consistency. Stir in vanilla.

boston babies

1 package (about 18 ounces) yellow cake mix
3 eggs *or* ¾ cup cholesterol-free egg substitute
⅓ cup unsweetened applesauce
1 package (4-serving size) sugar-free vanilla pudding and pie filling mix
2 cups low-fat (1%) milk or fat-free (skim) milk
1½ cups water
⅓ cup sugar
⅓ cup unsweetened cocoa powder
1 tablespoon cornstarch
1½ teaspoons vanilla

1. Line 24 (2½-inch) muffin pan cups with paper baking cups; set aside.

2. Prepare cake mix according to lower fat package directions, using 3 eggs and applesauce. Pour batter into prepared muffin cups. Bake according to package directions; cool completely. Freeze 12 cupcakes for another use.

3. Prepare pudding according to package directions, using 2 cups milk; cover and refrigerate.

4. For chocolate glaze, combine water, sugar, cocoa and cornstarch in large microwavable bowl; whisk until smooth. Microwave at HIGH 4 to 6 minutes, stirring every 2 minutes, until slightly thickened. Stir in vanilla.

5. To serve, for each dessert drizzle 2 tablespoons chocolate glaze on plate. Cut 1 cupcake in half; place halves on top of glaze. Top with about 2 heaping tablespoonfuls pudding. Garnish as desired. Serve immediately. *Makes 24 servings*

chocolate tiramisu cupcakes

Cupcakes

> 1 package (about 18 ounces) chocolate cake mix
> 1¼ cups water
> 3 eggs
> ⅓ cup vegetable oil or melted butter
> 2 tablespoons instant espresso powder
> 2 tablespoons brandy (optional)

Frosting

> 8 ounces mascarpone cheese or cream cheese
> 1½ to 1¾ cups powdered sugar
> 2 tablespoons coffee-flavored liqueur
> 1 tablespoon unsweetened cocoa powder

1. Preheat oven to 350°F. Line 30 regular-size (2½-inch) muffin cups with paper baking cups.

2. Beat all cupcake ingredients at low speed of electric mixer 30 seconds. Beat at medium speed 2 minutes.

3. Spoon batter into prepared muffin cups filling ⅔ full. Bake 20 to 22 minutes or until toothpicks inserted into centers come out clean. Cool in pans on wire racks 10 minutes. Remove cupcakes to racks; cool completely. (At this point, cupcakes may be frozen up to 3 months. Thaw at room temperature before frosting.)

4. For frosting, beat mascarpone cheese and 1½ cups powdered sugar at medium speed of electric mixer until well blended. Add liqueur; beat until well blended. If frosting is too soft, beat in additional powdered sugar or chill until spreadable.

5. Frost cooled cupcakes with frosting. Place cocoa in mesh strainer; shake over cupcakes. Store at room temperature up to 24 hours or cover and refrigerate for up to 3 days before serving.

Makes 30 cupcakes

pumpkin bundtings
with apple cider glaze

Cakes

> 1 package (about 18 ounces) spice cake mix
> 1 (16-ounce) can solid pumpkin or mashed sweet potatoes
> 1⅓ cups water
> 3 eggs
> ⅓ cup vegetable oil
> 1 teaspoon vanilla, butter and nut flavoring

Glaze

> 4 cups plus 2 tablespoons apple cider, divided
> 16 whole cloves
> 4 cinnamon sticks *or* 2 teaspoons ground cinnamon
> 1½ teaspoons cornstarch
> ¾ cup prepared caramel ice cream topping (optional)

1. Preheat oven to 350°F.

2. For cakes, grease bottoms and sides of 12 mini bundt pans; flour lightly. Combine all cake ingredients in large bowl; mix well. Spoon batter equally into pans. Bake 30 minutes or until toothpicks inserted into centers come out clean. Cool on wire racks 15 minutes. Remove cakes to racks; cool completely.

3. For glaze, combine 4 cups apple cider, cloves and cinnamon sticks in nonstick skillet; bring to a boil over high heat. Boil 7 minutes or until liquid has reduced to 1 cup. Meanwhile, in small bowl or cup, combine remaining 2 tablespoons apple cider and cornstarch; stir until cornstarch is dissolved.

4. When cider mixture is reduced, stir in cornstarch mixture; cook until slightly thickened, stirring constantly. Remove from heat; cool completely.

5. Remove and discard cloves and cinnamon from glaze. Spoon about 1 tablespoon glaze over top of each cake. Drizzle 1 tablespoon caramel topping around outer edge of each cake' if desired.

Makes 12 servings

pretty-in-pink peppermint cupcakes →

    1 package (about 18 ounces) white cake mix
    1$^1/_3$ cups water
    3 egg whites
    2 tablespoons vegetable oil or melted butter
    $^1/_2$ teaspoon peppermint extract
    3 to 4 drops red liquid food coloring
    1 container (16 ounces) prepared vanilla frosting
    $^1/_2$ cup crushed peppermint candies (about 16 candies)

Preheat oven to 350°F. Line 30 regular-size (2$^1/_2$-inch) muffin pan
cups with pink or white paper baking cups. Beat cake mix, water, egg
whites, oil, peppermint extract and food coloring until well blended.
Spoon batter into prepared muffin cups filling $^3/_4$ full. Bake 20 to
22 minutes or until toothpicks inserted into centers come out clean.
Cool in pans on wire racks 10 minutes. Remove cupcakes to racks; cool
completely. Spread cooled cupcakes with frosting; top with crushed
candies.   *Makes 30 cupcakes*

golden apple cupcakes

    1 package (18 to 20 ounces) yellow cake mix
    1 cup MOTT'S® Chunky Apple Sauce
    $^1/_3$ cup vegetable oil
    3 eggs
    $^1/_4$ cup firmly packed light brown sugar
    $^1/_4$ cup chopped walnuts
    $^1/_2$ teaspoon ground cinnamon
    Vanilla Frosting (recipe follows)

Heat oven to 350°F. In bowl, beat cake mix, apple sauce, oil and eggs
until well blended. Spoon batter into 24 paper-lined muffin pan cups.
Mix brown sugar, walnuts and cinnamon; sprinkle over batter in
muffin cups. Bake 20 to 25 minutes or until toothpick inserted in
center comes out clean. Cool in pan 10 minutes. Remove from pan;
cool completely on wire rack. Frost cupcakes with Vanilla Frosting.
                                                  Makes 24 cupcakes

vanilla frosting: In bowl, beat 1 package (8 ounces) softened cream
cheese until light and creamy; blend in $^1/_4$ teaspoon vanilla extract.
Beat $^1/_2$ cup heavy cream until stiff; fold into cream cheese mixture.

lemon poppy seed cupcakes

Cupcakes

    1 package.DUNCAN HINES® Moist Deluxe® Lemon Supreme
       Cake Mix

    3 eggs

  1$^1/_3$ cups water

   $^1/_3$ cup vegetable oil

    3 tablespoons poppy seed

Lemon Frosting

    1 container (16 ounces) DUNCAN HINES® Vanilla Frosting

    1 teaspoon grated lemon peel

  $^1/_4$ teaspoon lemon extract

    3 to 4 drops yellow food coloring

     Yellow and orange gumdrops for garnish

1. Preheat oven to 350°F. Place 30 (2½-inch) paper liners in muffin cups.

2. For cupcakes, combine cake mix, eggs, water, oil and poppy seed in large bowl. Beat at medium speed of electric mixer 2 minutes. Fill paper liners about half full. Bake 18 to 21 minutes or until toothpick inserted in center comes out clean. Cool in pans 5 minutes. Remove to cooling racks. Cool completely.

3. For lemon frosting, combine Vanilla frosting, lemon peel and lemon extract in small bowl. Tint with yellow food coloring to desired color. Frost cupcakes with lemon frosting. Decorate with gumdrops.

Makes 30 cupcakes

chocolate peanut butter cups →

    1 package DUNCAN HINES® Moist Deluxe® Swiss Chocolate
       Cake Mix
    1 container DUNCAN HINES® Creamy Home-Style Classic
       Vanilla Frosting
  $1/2$ cup creamy peanut butter
  15 miniature peanut butter cup candies, wrappers removed, cut in
       half vertically

1. Preheat oven to 350°F. Place 30 (2½-inch) paper liners in muffin cups.

2. Prepare, bake and cool cupcakes following package directions for basic recipe.

3. Combine Vanilla frosting and peanut butter in medium bowl. Stir until smooth. Frost one cupcake. Decorate with peanut butter cup candy, cut side down. Repeat with remaining cupcakes, frosting and candies.

Makes 30 servings

note: You can substitute Duncan Hines® Moist Deluxe® Devil's Food, Dark Chocolate Fudge or Butter Recipe Fudge Cake Mix flavors for Swiss Chocolate Cake Mix.

coconut cupcakes

    1 package DUNCAN HINES® Moist Deluxe® Butter Recipe Golden
       Cake Mix
    3 eggs
    1 cup (8 ounces) dairy sour cream
  $2/3$ cup cream of coconut
  $1/4$ cup butter or margarine, softened
    2 containers (16 ounces each) DUNCAN HINES® Coconut
       Frosting

1. Preheat oven to 375°F. Place 36 (2½-inch) paper liners in muffin cups.

2. Combine cake mix, eggs, sour cream, cream of coconut and butter in large bowl. Beat at low speed of electric mixer until blended. Beat at medium speed 4 minutes. Fill paper liners half full. Bake at 375°F for 17 to 19 minutes or until toothpick inserted into center comes out clean. Cool in pans 5 minutes. Remove to cooling racks. Cool completely.

3. Frost cupcakes.

Makes 36 cupcakes

cappuccino cupcakes

    1 package (about 18 ounces) dark chocolate cake mix
1¹/₃ cups strong brewed or instant coffee, at room temperature
    3 eggs
  ¹/₃ cup vegetable oil or melted butter
    1 container (16 ounces) vanilla frosting
    2 tablespoons coffee liqueur
      Additional coffee liqueur (optional)
      Grated chocolate*
      Chocolate-covered coffee beans (optional)

*Grate half of a 3- or 4-ounce milk, dark or espresso chocolate candy bar on the large holes of a grater.

1. Preheat oven to 350°F. Line 24 regular-size (2¹/₂-inch) muffin pan cups with foil or paper baking cups.

2. Beat cake mix, coffee, eggs and oil with electric mixer at low speed 30 seconds. Beat at medium speed 2 minutes.

3. Spoon batter into prepared muffin cups filling ²/₃ full. Bake 18 to 20 minutes or until toothpicks inserted into centers come out clean. Cool in pans on wire racks 10 minutes. Remove cupcakes to racks; cool completely. (At this point, cupcakes may be frozen up to 3 months. Thaw at room temperature before frosting.)

4. Combine frosting and 2 tablespoons liqueur in small bowl; mix well. Before frosting, poke about 10 holes in each cupcake with toothpick. Pour 1 to 2 teaspoons liqueur over top of each cupcake, if desired. Frost and sprinkle with grated chocolate. Garnish with chocolate-covered coffee beans, if desired.   *Makes 24 cupcakes*

chocolate petits fours

1 package DUNCAN HINES® Moist Deluxe® Dark Chocolate
    Fudge Cake Mix
1 package (7 ounces) pure almond paste
½ cup seedless red raspberry jam
3 cups semisweet chocolate chips
½ cup vegetable shortening plus additional for greasing

1. Preheat oven to 350°F. Grease and flour 13×9×2-inch pan.

2. Prepare, bake and cool cake following package directions for basic recipe. Remove from pan. Cover and store overnight (see hint). Level top of cake. Trim ¼-inch strip of cake from all sides. (Be careful to make straight cuts.) Cut cake into small squares, rectangles or triangles with serrated knife. Cut round and heart shapes with 1½- to 2-inch cookie cutters. Split each individual cake horizontally into two layers.

3. For filling, cut almond paste in half. Roll half the paste between two sheets of waxed paper to ⅛-inch thickness. Cut into same shapes as individual cakes. Repeat with second half of paste. Warm jam in small saucepan over low heat until thin. Remove top of one cake. Spread ¼ to ½ teaspoon jam on inside of each cut surface. Place one almond paste cutout on bottom layer. Top with second half of cake, jam side down. Repeat with remaining cakes.

4. For glaze, place chocolate chips and ½ cup shortening in 4-cup glass measuring cup. Microwave at MEDIUM (50% power) for 2 minutes; stir. Microwave for 2 minutes longer at MEDIUM; stir until smooth. Place 3 assembled cakes on cooling rack over bowl. Spoon chocolate glaze over each cake until top and sides are completely covered. Remove to waxed paper when glaze has stopped dripping. Repeat process until all cakes are covered. (Return chocolate glaze in bowl to glass measuring cup as needed; microwave at MEDIUM for 30 to 60 seconds to thin.)

5. Place remaining chocolate glaze in resealable plastic bag; seal. Place bag in bowl of hot water for several minutes. Dry with paper towel. Knead until chocolate is smooth. Snip pinpoint hole in bottom corner of bag. Drizzle or decorate top of each petit four. Let stand until chocolate is set. Store in single layer in airtight containers.

Makes 24 to 32 servings

hint: To make cutting the cake into shapes easier, bake the cake one day before assembling.

cherry cupcakes →

    1 (18¾-ounce) box chocolate cake mix
    3 eggs
    1⅓ cups water
    ½ cup vegetable oil
    1 (21-ounce) can cherry pie filling
    1 (16-ounce) can vanilla frosting

Prepare cake mix according to package directions, using eggs, water and oil. Pour batter into 24 paper-lined muffin-pan cups, filling two-thirds full.

Remove 24 cherries from cherry filling; set aside. Spoon generous teaspoon of remaining cherry filling onto center of each cupcake.

Bake in preheated 350°F oven 20 to 25 minutes. Cool in pans on wire racks 10 minutes. Remove from pan. Let cool completely. Frost cupcakes with vanilla frosting. Garnish cupcakes with reserved cherries.   *Makes 24 cupcakes*

Favorite recipe from **Cherry Marketing Institute**

quick & easy pumpkin cupcakes

    1 package (18.25 ounces) spice cake mix
    1 can (15 ounces) LIBBY'S® 100% Pure Pumpkin
    3 eggs
    ⅓ cup vegetable oil
    ⅓ cup water
    1 container (16 ounces) prepared cream cheese or vanilla
        frosting
    Assorted sprinkles

PREHEAT oven to 350°F. Paper-line or grease 24 muffin cups.

BLEND cake mix, pumpkin, eggs, vegetable oil and water in large mixer bowl until moistened. Beat on medium speed of electric mixer for 2 minutes. Pour batter into prepared muffin cups, filling ¾ full.

BAKE for 18 to 23 minutes or until wooden pick inserted in center comes out clean. Cool in pan on wire rack for 10 minutes; remove to wire racks to cool completely. Spread cupcakes with frosting. Decorate as desired.   *Makes 24 cupcakes*

charming
cookies

chocolate almond biscotti

1 package DUNCAN HINES® Moist Deluxe® Dark Chocolate
    Cake Mix
1 cup all-purpose flour
1/2 cup butter or margarine, melted
2 eggs
1 teaspoon almond extract
1/2 cup chopped almonds
    White chocolate, melted (optional)

1. Preheat oven to 350°F. Line 2 baking sheets with parchment paper.

2. Combine cake mix, flour, butter, eggs and almond extract in large bowl. Beat at low speed with electric mixer until well blended; stir in almonds. Divide dough in half. Shape each half into 12×2-inch log; place logs on prepared baking sheets. (Bake logs separately.)

3. Bake at 350°F for 30 to 35 minutes or until toothpick inserted in centers comes out clean. Remove logs from oven; cool on baking sheets 15 minutes. Using serrated knife, cut logs into 1/2-inch slices. Arrange slices on baking sheets. Bake biscotti 10 minutes. Remove to cooling racks; cool completely.

4. Dip one end of each biscotti in melted white chocolate, if desired. Allow white chocolate to set at room temperature before storing biscotti in airtight container. *Makes about 2 1/2 dozen cookies*

White chocolate is more delicate than other chocolates and burns easily. Melt it carefully in a double boiler over simmering water and stir constantly.

spicy oatmeal raisin cookies →

    1 package DUNCAN HINES® Moist Deluxe® Spice Cake Mix
    4 egg whites
    1 cup uncooked quick-cooking oats (not instant or
        old-fashioned)
    ¹/₂ cup vegetable oil
    ¹/₂ cup raisins

1. Preheat oven to 350°F. Grease baking sheets.

2. Combine cake mix, egg whites, oats and oil in large mixing bowl.
Beat at low speed with electric mixer until blended. Stir in raisins.
Drop by rounded teaspoonfuls onto prepared baking sheets.

3. Bake at 350°F for 7 to 9 minutes or until lightly browned. Cool
1 minute on baking sheets. Remove to cooling racks; cool completely.

Makes about 4 dozen cookies

triple chocolate cookies

    1 package DUNCAN HINES® Moist Deluxe® Swiss Chocolate
        Cake Mix
    ¹/₂ cup butter or margarine, melted
    1 egg
    ¹/₂ cup semisweet chocolate chips
    ¹/₂ cup milk chocolate chips
    ¹/₂ cup coarsely chopped white chocolate
    ¹/₂ cup chopped pecans

1. Preheat oven to 375°F.

2. Combine cake mix, melted butter and egg in large bowl. Beat at low
speed with electric mixer until blended. Stir in all 3 chocolates and
pecans.

3. Drop by rounded tablespoonfuls onto ungreased baking sheets.
Bake at 375°F for 9 to 11 minutes. Cool 1 minute on baking sheets.
Remove to cooling racks. *Makes 3¹/₂ to 4 dozen cookies*

note: Cookies can be stored in an airtight container in freezer for up to
6 months.

lemon cookies →

    1 package DUNCAN HINES® Moist Deluxe® Lemon Supreme
      Cake Mix
    2 eggs
    1/3 cup vegetable oil
    1 tablespoon lemon juice
    3/4 cup chopped nuts or flaked coconut
      Confectioners' sugar

1. Preheat oven to 375°F. Grease baking sheets.

2. Combine cake mix, eggs, oil and lemon juice in large bowl. Beat at low speed with electric mixer until well blended. Add nuts. Shape dough into 1-inch balls. Place 1 inch apart on prepared baking sheets.

3. Bake at 375°F for 6 to 7 minutes or until lightly browned. Cool 1 minute on baking sheets. Remove to cooling racks. Sprinkle with confectioners' sugar. *Makes about 3 dozen cookies*

note: You can frost cookies with 1 cup confectioners' sugar mixed with 1 tablespoon lemon juice instead of sprinkling cookies with confectioners' sugar.

butterscotch spice cookies

    1 package DUNCAN HINES® Moist Deluxe® Spice Cake Mix
    2 eggs
    1/2 cup vegetable oil
    1 teaspoon vanilla extract
    1 cup butterscotch flavored chips

1. Preheat oven to 375°F.

2. Combine cake mix, eggs, oil and vanilla extract in large bowl. Beat at low speed with electric mixer until blended. Stir in butterscotch chips. Drop by rounded teaspoonfuls 2 inches apart onto ungreased baking sheets. Bake at 375°F for 8 to 10 minutes or until set. Cool 2 minutes on baking sheets. Remove to cooling racks. Cool completely. Store in airtight container. *Makes 3 dozen cookies*

hint: For chewy cookies, bake for 8 minutes. Cookies will be slightly puffed when removed from the oven and will settle while cooling.

chocolate cherry cookies

1 package (8 ounces) low-fat sugar-free chocolate cake mix
3 tablespoons fat-free (skim) milk
1/2 teaspoon almond extract
10 maraschino cherries, rinsed, drained and cut into halves
2 tablespoons white chocolate chips
1/2 teaspoon vegetable oil

1. Preheat oven to 350°F. Spray cookie sheets with nonstick cooking spray; set aside.

2. Beat cake mix, milk and almond extract in medium bowl with electric mixer at low speed. Increase speed to medium when mixture looks crumbly; beat 2 minutes or until smooth dough forms. (Dough will be very sticky.)

3. Coat hands with cooking spray. Shape dough into 1-inch balls. Place balls 2 1/2 inches apart on prepared cookie sheets. Flatten each ball slightly. Place cherry half in center of each cookie.

4. Bake 8 to 9 minutes or until cookies lose their shininess and tops begin to crack. *Do not overbake.* Remove to wire racks; cool completely.

5. Heat white chocolate chips and oil in small saucepan over very low heat until chips melt. Drizzle cookies with melted chips. Allow drizzle to set before serving.   *Makes 20 cookies*

 The best cookie sheets to use are those with little or no sides. They allow the heat to circulate easily during baking and promote even browning.

chocolate chip 'n oatmeal cookies →

    1 package (18.25 or 18.5 ounces) yellow cake mix
    1 cup quick-cooking rolled oats, uncooked
    ³/₄ cup butter or margarine, softened
    2 eggs
    1 cup HERSHEY₃'S Semi-Sweet Chocolate Chips

1. Heat oven to 350°F.

2. Combine cake mix, oats, butter and eggs in large bowl; mix well. Stir in chocolate chips. Drop by rounded teaspoons onto ungreased cookie sheets.

3. Bake 10 to 12 minutes or until very lightly browned. Cool slightly; remove from cookie sheets to wire racks. Cool completely.

Makes about 4 dozen cookies

devil's food fudge cookies

    1 package DUNCAN HINES® Moist Deluxe® Devil's Food
        Cake Mix
    2 eggs
    ¹/₂ cup vegetable oil
    1 cup semisweet chocolate chips
    ¹/₂ cup chopped walnuts

1. Preheat oven to 350°F. Grease baking sheets.

2. Combine cake mix, eggs and oil in large bowl. Stir until thoroughly blended. Stir in chocolate chips and walnuts. (Mixture will be stiff.) Shape dough into 36 (1¹/₄-inch) balls. Place 2 inches apart on prepared baking sheets.

3. Bake at 350°F for 10 to 11 minutes. (Cookies will look moist.) *Do not overbake.* Cool 2 minutes on baking sheets. Remove to cooling racks. Cool completely. Store in airtight container.

Makes 3 dozen cookies

variation: For a delicious flavor treat, substitute peanut butter chips for the chocolate chips and chopped peanuts for the chopped walnuts.

cinnamon stars

2 tablespoons sugar
$^3/_4$ teaspoon ground cinnamon
$^3/_4$ cup butter or margarine, softened
2 egg yolks
1 teaspoon vanilla extract
1 package DUNCAN HINES® Moist Deluxe® French Vanilla
    Cake Mix

1. Preheat oven to 375°F. Combine sugar and cinnamon in small bowl. Set aside.

2. Combine butter, egg yolks and vanilla extract in large bowl. Blend in cake mix gradually. Roll dough to $^1/_8$-inch thickness on lightly floured surface. Cut with 2$^1/_2$-inch star cookie cutter. Place 2 inches apart on ungreased baking sheet.

3. Sprinkle cookies with cinnamon-sugar mixture. Bake at 375°F for 6 to 8 minutes or until edges are light golden brown. Cool 1 minute on baking sheet. Remove to cooling rack. Cool completely. Store in airtight container. *Makes 3 to 3$^1/_2$ dozen cookies*

variation: You can use your favorite cookie cutter in place of the star cookie cutter.

For easier handling, chill cookie dough before rolling. Remove only enough dough from the refrigerator to work with at one time. Save any scraps and reroll them all at once to prevent the dough from becoming tough.

crispy thumbprint cookies

1 package (about 18 ounces) yellow cake mix
$^1\!/_2$ cup vegetable oil
$^1\!/_4$ cup water
1 egg
3 cups crisp rice cereal, crushed
$^1\!/_2$ cup chopped walnuts
6 tablespoons raspberry or strawberry preserves

1. Preheat oven to 375°F.

2. Combine cake mix, oil, water and egg. Beat at medium speed of electric mixer until well blended. Add cereal and walnuts; stir until well blended.

3. Drop by heaping teaspoonfuls about 2 inches apart onto ungreased baking sheets. Use thumb to make indentation in each cookie. Spoon about $^1\!/_2$ teaspoon preserves into center of each cookie.

4. Bake 9 to 11 minutes or until golden brown. Cool cookies 1 minute on baking sheet. Remove to wire rack; cool completely.

Makes 3 dozen cookies

Prep and Cook Time: 30 minutes

choco-scutterbotch

$^2/_3$ **Butter Flavor CRISCO® Stick or $^2/_3$ cup Butter Flavor CRISCO®**
   all-vegetable shortening
$^1/_2$ **cup firmly packed light brown sugar**
 2 eggs
 1 package (18$^1/_4$ ounces) deluxe yellow cake mix
 1 cup toasted rice cereal
$^1/_2$ **cup butterscotch chips**
$^1/_2$ **cup milk chocolate chunks**
$^1/_2$ **cup semisweet chocolate chips**
$^1/_2$ **cup coarsely chopped walnuts or pecans**

1. Heat oven to 375°F. Place sheets of foil on countertop for cooling cookies.

2. Combine $^2/_3$ cup shortening and brown sugar in large bowl. Beat at medium speed of electric mixer until well blended. Beat in eggs.

3. Add cake mix gradually at low speed. Mix until well blended. Stir in cereal, butterscotch chips, chocolate chunks, chocolate chips and nuts. Stir until well blended.

4. Shape dough into 1$^1/_4$-inch balls. Place 2 inches apart on ungreased baking sheet. Flatten slightly. Shape sides to form circle, if necessary.

5. Bake for 7 to 9 minutes or until lightly browned around edges. *Do not overbake.* Cool 2 minutes on baking sheet. Remove cookies to foil to cool completely. *Makes 3 dozen cookies*

coconut clouds

2²/₃ cups flaked coconut, divided
1 package DUNCAN HINES® Moist Deluxe® Classic Yellow
    Cake Mix
1 egg
¹/₂ cup vegetable oil
¹/₄ cup water
1 teaspoon almond extract

1. Preheat oven to 350°F. Reserve 1¹/₃ cups coconut in medium bowl; set aside.

2. Combine cake mix, egg, oil, water and almond extract in large bowl. Beat at low speed with electric mixer. Stir in remaining 1¹/₃ cups coconut. Drop rounded teaspoonful dough into reserved coconut. Roll to cover lightly. Place on ungreased baking sheet. Repeat with remaining dough, placing balls 2 inches apart. Bake at 350°F for 10 to 12 minutes or until light golden brown. Cool 1 minute on baking sheets. Remove to cooling racks. Cool completely. Store in airtight container. *Makes 3¹/₂ dozen cookies*

To save time when dropping dough onto the baking sheet, use a 1-inch spring-operated cookie scoop. They can be purchased at kitchen specialty shops.

chocolate peanut butter cookies →

>1 package DUNCAN HINES® Moist Deluxe® Devil's Food
>   Cake Mix
>¾ cup crunchy peanut butter
>2 eggs
>2 tablespoons milk
>1 cup candy-coated peanut butter pieces

1. Preheat oven to 350°F. Grease baking sheets.

2. Combine cake mix, peanut butter, eggs and milk in large mixing bowl. Beat at low speed with electric mixer until blended. Stir in peanut butter pieces.

3. Drop dough by slightly rounded tablespoonfuls onto prepared baking sheets. Bake 7 to 9 minutes or until lightly browned. Cool 2 minutes on baking sheets. Remove to cooling racks.

Makes about 3½ dozen cookies

swiss chocolate crispies

>1 package DUNCAN HINES® Moist Deluxe® Swiss Chocolate
>   Cake Mix
>½ cup shortening plus additional for greasing
>½ cup butter or margarine, softened
>2 eggs
>2 tablespoons water
>3 cups crispy rice cereal, divided

1. Combine cake mix, ½ cup shortening, butter, eggs and water in large bowl. Beat at low speed with electric mixer for 2 minutes. Fold in 1 cup cereal. Refrigerate 1 hour.

2. Crush remaining 2 cups cereal into coarse crumbs.

3. Preheat oven to 350°F. Grease baking sheets. Shape dough into 1-inch balls. Roll in crushed cereal. Place on baking sheets about 1 inch apart.

4. Bake at 350°F for 11 to 13 minutes. Cool 1 minute on baking sheets. Remove to wire racks.

Makes about 4 dozen cookies

easy lemon cookies →

1 package DUNCAN HINES® Moist Deluxe® Lemon Cake Mix
2 eggs
1/2 cup vegetable oil
1 teaspoon grated lemon peel
Pecan halves for garnish

1. Preheat oven to 350°F.

2. Combine cake mix, eggs, oil and lemon peel in large bowl. Stir until thoroughly blended. Drop by rounded teaspoonfuls 2 inches apart onto ungreased baking sheets. Press pecan half into center of each cookie. Bake at 350°F for 9 to 11 minutes or until edges are light golden brown. Cool 1 minute on baking sheets. Remove to wire racks. Cool completely. Store in airtight container. *Makes 4 dozen cookies*

note: You can substitute whole almonds or walnut halves for the pecan halves.

quick peanut butter chocolate chip cookies

1 package DUNCAN HINES® Moist Deluxe® Classic Yellow
   Cake Mix
1/2 cup creamy peanut butter
1/2 cup butter or margarine, softened
2 eggs
1 cup milk chocolate chips

1. Preheat oven to 350°F. Grease baking sheets.

2. Combine cake mix, peanut butter, butter and eggs in large bowl. Mix at low speed with electric mixer until blended. Stir in chocolate chips.

3. Drop by rounded teaspoonfuls onto prepared baking sheets. Bake at 350°F for 9 to 11 minutes or until lightly browned. Cool 2 minutes on baking sheets. Remove to cooling racks.

Makes about 4 dozen cookies

note: Crunchy peanut butter can be substituted for regular peanut butter.

caramel pecan cookies

Cookie
   $^{1}/_{2}$ **Butter Flavor CRISCO® Stick or $^{1}/_{2}$ cup Butter Flavor CRISCO®**
      all-vegetable shortening, melted
   1 package (18.25 ounces) yellow cake mix
   1 cup JIF® Crunchy Peanut Butter
   2 tablespoons orange juice or water
   2 eggs

Caramel and Chocolate Topping
   28 caramels
   2 tablespoons milk
   2 cups pecan halves
   1 package (6 ounces) semisweet chocolate chips

1. Heat oven to 350°F. Place sheets of foil on countertop for cooling cookies.

2. For cookie, combine shortening, cake mix, peanut butter, juice and eggs in large bowl. Beat at medium speed of electric mixer until well blended.

3. Drop rounded tablespoonfuls of dough, 3 inches apart, onto ungreased baking sheet.

4. Bake at 350°F for 10 to 12 minutes, or until set. *Do not overbake.* Cool 2 minutes on baking sheet. Remove cookies to foil to cool completely.

5. For topping, combine caramels and milk in microwave-safe bowl. Cover with waxed paper. Microwave at 50% (MEDIUM). Stir after 1 minute. Repeat until smooth (or melt on rangetop in small saucepan on very low heat). Drop rounded teaspoonfuls on top of each cookie. Place 3 pecan halves around edge of caramel to resemble turtles.

6. Place chocolate chips in microwave-safe cup. Microwave at 50% (MEDIUM). Stir after 1 minute. Repeat until smooth (or melt on rangetop in small saucepan on very low heat). Spread rounded teaspoonfuls over top of caramel, but do not cover the pecans. Cool completely. *Makes about 4 dozen cookies*

vanilla butter crescents

1 package DUNCAN HINES® Moist Deluxe® French Vanilla
    Cake Mix
³/₄ cup butter, softened
1 vanilla bean, very finely chopped (see tip)
1 cup finely chopped pecans or walnuts
    Confectioners' sugar

1. Preheat oven to 350°F.

2. Place cake mix and butter in large bowl. Cut in butter with pastry blender or 2 knives. Stir in vanilla bean and pecans. Since mixture is crumbly, it may be helpful to work dough with hands to blend until mixture holds together. Shape dough into balls. Roll 1 ball between palms until 4 inches long. Shape into crescent. Repeat with remaining balls. Place 2 inches apart on ungreased baking sheets.

3. Bake at 350°F for 10 to 12 minutes or until light golden brown around edges. Cool 2 minutes on baking sheets. Remove to cooling racks.

4. Dust with confectioners' sugar; cool completely. Dust with additional confectioners' sugar, if desired. Store in airtight container.

Makes 4 dozen cookies

To quickly chop the vanilla bean, place it in the work bowl of a food processor that is fitted with the knife blade. Process until finely chopped.

abracadabra bars

strawberry streusel squares

1 package (about 18 ounces) yellow cake mix, divided
3 tablespoons uncooked old-fashioned oats
1 tablespoon margarine
1 1/2 cups sliced strawberries
3/4 cup plus 2 tablespoons water, divided
3/4 cup diced strawberries
3 egg whites
1/3 cup unsweetened applesauce
1/2 teaspoon ground cinnamon
1/8 teaspoon ground nutmeg

1. Preheat oven to 350°F. Lightly grease and flour 13×9-inch baking pan.

2. Combine 1/2 cup cake mix and oats in small bowl. Cut in margarine until mixture resembles coarse crumbs; set aside.

3. Place 1 1/2 cups sliced strawberries and 2 tablespoons water in blender or food processor. Process until smooth. Transfer to small bowl and stir in 3/4 cup diced strawberries; set aside.

4. Place remaining cake mix in large bowl. Add 3/4 cup water, egg whites, applesauce, cinnamon and nutmeg. Blend 30 seconds at low speed of electric mixer or just until moistened. Beat at medium speed 2 minutes. Pour batter into prepared pan.

5. Spoon strawberry mixture evenly over batter, spreading lightly. Sprinkle evenly with oat mixture. Bake 31 to 34 minutes or until toothpick inserted into center comes out clean. Cool completely in pan on wire rack. Cut into squares. *Makes 12 servings*

lemon crumb bars

1 (18.25-ounce) package lemon or yellow cake mix
$\frac{1}{2}$ cup (1 stick) butter or margarine, softened
1 egg
2 cups finely crushed saltine cracker crumbs
3 egg yolks
1 (14-ounce) can EAGLE BRAND® Sweetened Condensed Milk
    (NOT evaporated milk)
$\frac{1}{2}$ cup lemon juice from concentrate

1. Preheat oven to 350°F. Grease 15×10×1-inch baking pan. In large mixing bowl, combine cake mix, butter and 1 egg; mix well (mixture will be crumbly). Stir in cracker crumbs. Reserve 2 cups crumb mixture. Press remaining crumb mixture firmly on bottom of prepared pan. Bake 15 minutes.

2. Meanwhile, in medium mixing bowl, combine egg yolks, Eagle Brand and lemon juice; mix well. Spread evenly over baked crust.

3. Top with reserved crumb mixture. Bake 20 minutes or until firm. Cool. Cut into bars. Store covered in refrigerator.

Makes 3 to 4 dozen bars

Prep Time: 30 minutes
Bake Time: 35 minutes

To quickly soften butter, place 1 stick of butter on a microwavable plate and heat at LOW (30% power) about 30 seconds or just until softened.

chocolate caramel nut bars

 1 package (about 18 ounces) devil's food cake mix
 ³/₄ cup (1¹/₂ sticks) butter, melted
 ¹/₂ cup milk, divided
 60 vanilla caramels
 1 cup cashews, coarsely chopped
 1 cup semisweet chocolate chips

Preheat oven to 350°F. Grease 13×9-inch baking pan. Combine cake mix, butter and ¹/₄ cup milk in medium bowl; mix well. Spread half of batter into bottom of prepared pan.

Bake 7 to 8 minutes or until batter just begins to form crust. Remove from oven.

Meanwhile, combine caramels and remaining ¹/₄ cup milk in heavy medium saucepan. Cook over low heat, stirring often, about 5 minutes or until caramels are melted and mixture is smooth.

Pour melted caramel mixture over partially baked crust. Combine cashews and chocolate chips in small bowl; sprinkle over caramel mixture.

Drop spoonfuls of remaining batter evenly over nut mixture. Return pan to oven; bake 18 to 20 minutes more or until top cake layer springs back when lightly touched. (Caramel center will be soft.) Let cool on wire rack before cutting into squares or bars. (Bars can be frozen; let thaw 20 to 25 minutes before serving.)

Makes about 48 bars

Dish: Bar Cookies — Recipe — Serves:

Chocolate - Caramel - Nut Bars
1 package (18¼ ounces) devil's food cake mix
¼ cup butter or margarine, melted
½ cup milk, divided
60 vanilla caramels
1 cup cashew pieces, coarsely chopped
1 cup semisweet chocolate chips

PREHEAT oven to 350° F. Grease 13x9-inch ba...
Combine cake mix, butter and ¼ cup milk in m...

orange coconut cream bars →

1 (18¼-ounce) package yellow cake mix
1 cup quick-cooking or old-fashioned oats, uncooked
¾ cup chopped nuts
½ cup butter or margarine, melted
1 egg
1 (14-ounce) can sweetened condensed milk
2 teaspoons grated orange zest
1 cup shredded coconut
1 cup "M&M's"® Semi-Sweet Chocolate Mini Baking Bits

Preheat oven to 375°F. Lightly grease 13×9×2-inch baking pan; set aside. In large bowl combine cake mix, oats, nuts, butter and egg until ingredients are thoroughly moistened and mixture resembles coarse crumbs. Reserve 1 cup mixture. Firmly press remaining mixture onto bottom of prepared pan; bake 10 minutes. In separate bowl combine condensed milk and orange zest; spread over baked base. Combine reserved crumb mixture, coconut and "M&M's"® Semi-Sweet Chocolate Mini Baking Bits; sprinkle evenly over condensed milk mixture and press in lightly. Continue baking 20 to 25 minutes or until golden brown. Cool completely. Cut into bars. Store in tightly covered container. *Makes 26 bars*

butterscotch pan cookies

1 package DUNCAN HINES® Moist Deluxe® French Vanilla
  Cake Mix
2 eggs
1 cup butter or margarine, melted
¾ cup firmly packed light brown sugar
1 teaspoon vanilla extract
1 package (12 ounces) butterscotch flavored chips
1½ cups chopped pecans

1. Preheat oven to 375°F. Grease 15½×10½×1-inch jelly-roll pan.

2. Combine cake mix, eggs, melted butter, brown sugar and vanilla extract in large bowl. Beat at low speed with electric mixer until smooth and creamy. Stir in butterscotch chips and pecans. Spread in prepared pan. Bake at 375°F for 20 to 25 minutes or until golden brown. Cool completely. Cut into bars. *Makes 48 bars*

cherry spice bars

1 (10-ounce) jar maraschino cherries
1 (18¼-ounce) package spice cake mix
¼ cup butter or margarine, melted
¼ cup firmly packed brown sugar
¼ cup water
2 eggs

Glaze

1 cup confectioners' sugar
1 tablespoon lemon juice
1 to 2 teaspoons milk

Drain maraschino cherries; discard juice or save for another use. Cut cherries in half. Combine dry cake mix, melted butter, brown sugar, water and eggs in large mixing bowl; mix with spoon or electric mixer until well combined and smooth. Stir in maraschino cherries. Spread batter into greased 13×9×2-inch baking pan.

Bake in preheated 375°F oven 20 to 25 minutes, or until top springs back when lightly touched. Let cool in pan on wire rack.

For glaze, combine confectioners' sugar and lemon juice; add enough milk to make thick glaze. Drizzle glaze over cake. Allow glaze to set. Cut into bars. Store, up to one week, in airtight container with sheets of waxed paper between each layer of bars.   *Makes 2 dozen bars*

*Favorite recipe from **Cherry Marketing Institute***

chocolate macaroon squares

    1 package (18.25 ounce) chocolate cake mix
    $^1/_3$ cup butter or margarine, softened
    1 egg, lightly beaten
    1 can (14 ounces) NESTLÉ® CARNATION® Sweetened Condensed
       Milk
    1 egg
    1 teaspoon vanilla extract
    $1^1/_3$ cups flaked sweetened coconut, *divided*
    1 cup chopped pecans
    1 cup (6-ounce package) NESTLÉ® TOLL HOUSE® Semi-Sweet
       Chocolate Morsels

PREHEAT oven to 350°F.

COMBINE cake mix, butter and egg in large bowl; mix with fork until crumbly. Press onto bottom of ungreased 13×9-inch baking pan. Combine sweetened condensed milk, egg and vanilla extract in medium bowl; beat until well blended. Stir in *1 cup* coconut, nuts and morsels.

SPREAD mixture evenly over base; sprinkle with *remaining* coconut. Bake for 28 to 30 minutes or until center is almost set (center will firm when cool). Cool in pan on wire rack.   *Makes 24 squares*

lemon cheese bars →

1 package (about 18 ounces) white or yellow cake mix with
      pudding in the mix
2 eggs divided
$\frac{1}{3}$ cup vegetable oil
1 package (8 ounces) cream cheese
$\frac{1}{3}$ cup sugar
1 teaspoon lemon juice

1. Preheat oven to 350°F.

2. Combine cake mix, 1 egg and oil in large bowl until crumbly.
Reserve 1 cup cake mixture; press remaining mixture into ungreased
13×9-inch cake pan. Bake 15 minutes or until light golden brown.

3. Beat remaining egg, cream cheese, sugar and lemon juice until light
in color and smooth. Spread over baked layer. Sprinkle with reserved
cake mixture. Bake for an additional 15 minutes. Cool in pan on wire
rack; cut into bars.   *Makes 18 bars*

buckeye cookie bars

1 (18.25-ounce) package chocolate cake mix
$\frac{1}{4}$ cup vegetable oil
1 egg
1 cup chopped peanuts
1 (14-ounce) can EAGLE BRAND® Sweetened Condensed Milk
      (NOT evaporated milk)
$\frac{1}{2}$ cup peanut butter

1. Preheat oven to 350°F. In large mixing bowl, combine cake mix,
oil and egg; beat at medium speed of electric mixer until crumbly. Stir
in peanuts. Reserve 1$\frac{1}{2}$ cups crumb mixture; press remaining crumb
mixture firmly on bottom of greased 13×9-inch baking pan.

2. In medium mixing bowl, beat Eagle Brand with peanut butter until
smooth; spread over prepared crust. Sprinkle with reserved crumb
mixture.

3. Bake 25 to 30 minutes or until set. Cool. Cut into bars. Store
loosely covered at room temperature.   *Makes 24 to 36 bars*

double chocolate chewies

1 package DUNCAN HINES® Moist Deluxe® Butter Recipe Fudge
    Cake Mix
2 eggs
$^{1}/_{2}$ cup butter or margarine, melted
1 package (6 ounces) semisweet chocolate chips
1 cup chopped nuts
    Confectioners' sugar (optional)

1. Preheat oven to 350°F. Grease 13×9×2-inch pan.

2. Combine cake mix, eggs and melted butter in large bowl. Stir until
thoroughly blended. (Mixture will be stiff.) Stir in chocolate chips and
nuts. Press mixture evenly in prepared pan. Bake at 350°F for 25 to
30 minutes or until toothpick inserted in center comes out clean. *Do
not overbake.* Cool completely. Cut into bars. Dust with confectioners'
sugar, if desired. *Makes 36 bars*

serving suggestion: For a special effect, cut a paper towel into
$^{1}/_{4}$-inch-wide strips. Place strips in diagonal pattern on top of cooled
bars before cutting. Place confectioners' sugar in tea strainer. Tap
strainer lightly to dust surface with sugar. Carefully remove strips.

*For easy removal of bar cookies, line the pan with foil and
leave at least 3 inches hanging over each end. Use the foil
to lift out the treats, place them on a cutting board and
carefully remove the foil. Then simply cut them into bars.*

apricot crumb squares

1 package (about 18 ounces) light yellow cake mix
1 teaspoon ground cinnamon
$^{1}/_{2}$ teaspoon ground nutmeg
6 tablespoons cold butter, cut into pieces
$^{3}/_{4}$ cup uncooked multigrain oatmeal cereal or old-fashioned oats
1 whole egg
2 egg whites
1 tablespoon water
1 jar (10 ounces) apricot fruit spread
2 tablespoons packed light brown sugar

Preheat oven to 350°F. Combine cake mix, cinnamon and nutmeg in medium bowl. Cut in butter with pastry blender or 2 knives until coarse crumbs form. Stir in cereal. Reserve 1 cup mixture. Add whole egg, egg whites and water to remaining mixture; stir until well blended.

Spread batter evenly in ungreased 13×9-inch baking pan; top with fruit spread. Sprinkle reserved 1 cup cereal mixture over fruit; sprinkle with brown sugar.

Bake 35 to 40 minutes or until top is golden brown. Cool in pan on wire rack; cut into squares. *Makes 15 squares*

pecan date bars

Crust

> 1/3 **cup shortening plus additional for greasing**
> 1 **package DUNCAN HINES® Moist Deluxe® Classic White**
>   **Cake Mix**
> 1 **egg**

Topping

> 1 **package (8 ounces) chopped dates**
> 1 1/4 **cups chopped pecans**
> 1 **cup water**
> 1/2 **teaspoon vanilla extract**
>   **Confectioners' sugar**

1. Preheat oven to 350°F. Grease and flour 13×9-inch baking pan.

2. For crust, cut 1/3 cup shortening into cake mix with pastry blender or 2 knives until mixture resembles coarse crumbs. Add egg; stir well (mixture will be crumbly). Press mixture into bottom of prepared pan.

3. For topping, combine dates, pecans and water in medium saucepan. Bring to a boil. Reduce heat; simmer until mixture thickens, stirring constantly. Remove from heat. Stir in vanilla extract. Spread date mixture evenly over crust. Bake at 350°F for 25 to 30 minutes. Cool completely. Dust with confectioners' sugar.

Makes about 32 bars

lemon bars

1 package DUNCAN HINES® Moist Deluxe® Lemon Supreme
   Cake Mix
3 eggs, divided
$1/3$ cup butter-flavor shortening
$1/2$ cup granulated sugar
$1/4$ cup lemon juice
2 teaspoons grated lemon peel
$1/2$ teaspoon baking powder
$1/4$ teaspoon salt
   Confectioners' sugar

1. Preheat oven to 350°F.

2. Combine cake mix, 1 egg and shortening in large mixing bowl. Beat at low speed with electric mixer until crumbs form. Reserve 1 cup. Pat remaining mixture lightly into *ungreased* 13×9-inch pan. Bake at 350°F for 15 minutes or until lightly browned.

3. Combine remaining 2 eggs, granulated sugar, lemon juice, lemon peel, baking powder and salt in medium mixing bowl. Beat at medium speed with electric mixer until light and foamy. Pour over hot crust. Sprinkle with reserved crumb mixture.

4. Bake at 350°F for 15 minutes or until lightly browned. Sprinkle with confectioners' sugar. Cool in pan. Cut into bars.

Makes 30 to 32 bars

note: These bars are also delicious using Duncan Hines® Moist Deluxe® Classic Yellow Cake Mix.

double chocolate fantasy bars

1 (18.25-ounce) package chocolate cake mix
¼ cup vegetable oil
1 egg
1 cup chopped nuts
1 (14-ounce) can EAGLE BRAND® Sweetened Condensed Milk
(NOT evaporated milk)
1 (6-ounce) package semi-sweet chocolate chips
1 teaspoon vanilla extract
Dash salt

1. Preheat oven to 350°F. Grease 13×9-inch baking pan. In large mixing bowl, combine cake mix, oil and egg; beat at medium speed until crumbly. Stir in nuts. Reserve 1½ cups crumb mixture. Press remaining crumb mixture firmly on bottom of prepared pan.

2. In small saucepan over medium heat, combine remaining ingredients. Cook and stir until chips melt.

3. Pour chocolate mixture evenly over prepared crust. Sprinkle reserved crumb mixture evenly over top. Bake 25 to 30 minutes or until set. Cool. Cut into bars. Store loosely covered at room temperature. *Makes 36 bars*

Prep Time: 15 minutes
Bake Time: 25 to 30 minutes

 Most bar cookies should cool in the pan on a wire rack until barely warm before cutting. Try cutting bar cookies into triangles or diamonds for a festive new shape.

banana gingerbread bars

 1 package (14.5 ounces) gingerbread cake mix
 $\frac{1}{2}$ cup lukewarm water
 1 ripe, medium DOLE® Banana, mashed (about $\frac{1}{2}$ cup)
 1 egg
 1 small DOLE® Banana, peeled and chopped
 $\frac{1}{2}$ cup DOLE® Seedless Raisins
 $\frac{1}{2}$ cup slivered almonds
 $1\frac{1}{2}$ cups powdered sugar
    Juice from 1 lemon

• Preheat oven to 350°F.

• In large mixer bowl, combine gingerbread mix, water, mashed banana and egg. Beat on low speed of electric mixer 1 minute.

• Stir in chopped banana, raisins and almonds.

• Spread batter in greased 13×9-inch baking pan. Bake 20 to 25 minutes or until top springs back when lightly touched.

• In medium bowl, mix powdered sugar and 3 tablespoons lemon juice to make thin glaze. Spread over warm gingerbread. Cool before cutting into bars. Sprinkle with additional powdered sugar, if desired.

Makes about 32 bars

acknowledgments

*The publisher would like to thank the companies and organizations
listed below for the use of their recipes and photographs
in this publication.*

Cherry Marketing Institute

Dole Food Company, Inc.

Duncan Hines® and Moist Deluxe® are registered trademarks of
Aurora Foods Inc.

Eagle Brand®

Filippo Berio® Olive Oil

Hershey Foods Corporation

Kahlúa® Liqueur

© Mars, Incorporated 2004

McIlhenny Company (TABASCO® brand Pepper Sauce)

Mott's® is a registered trademark of Mott's, Inc.

Nestlé USA

The Quaker® Oatmeal Kitchens

The J.M. Smucker Company

Reprinted with permission of Sunkist Growers, Inc.

Unilever Bestfoods North America